NATURE PATTERNS

Compiled by Jean Warren

Illustrated by Gary Mohrmann

Warren Publishing House, Inc.
Everett, Washington

Editorial Staff: Gayle Bittinger, Susan M. Sexton, Jean Warren

Production Director: Eileen Carbary

Design: Kathy Jones

Cover–Computer Graphics: Kathy Jones and André Gene Samson

Inside Pages–Text and Computer Graphics: André Gene Samson

ISBN: 0-911019-36-7

Printed in the United States of America
Published by: Warren Publishing House, Inc.
P.O. Box 2250
Everett, Washington 98203

CONTENTS

Using Nature Patterns

Mix and match the patterns in this book to create a variety of teaching props, learning games, bulletin boards and more. Following are some suggestions of ways to use the patterns. Adapt these ideas or make up you own — the only limit is your imagination.

Language

Flannelboard Story Characters—Use the patterns as guides to cut nature shapes out of felt or construction paper backed with felt strips.

Stick Puppets—Color and cut out photocopies of the smallest nature shapes and glue them to Popsicle sticks or tongue depressors.

Stand-up Story Characters—Use the patterns as guides to cut nature shapes out of posterboard. Make stands for the shapes out of posterboard or playdough.

Magnetic Story Character—Use the patterns as guides to cut nature shapes out of construction paper or posterboard and attach magnets to the backs of them.

Picture Books—Photocopy several nature shapes of the same size, arrange them in the desired order and staple them together to make books. Add construction paper covers, if desired.

Draw-A-Story—Cut out several photocopied shapes, cover them with clear self-stick paper and put them in a bag or a box. Let the children take turns pulling out a shape for you to incorporate into a story.

Music and Movement

Finger Puppets—Color and cut out photocopies of the smallest nature shapes and attach them to construction paper or pipe cleaner "rings." Use the finger puppets while reciting poems or singing nature songs.

Nature Songs—Use the patterns as guides to cut nature shapes out of construction paper or felt. Use the shapes as props while singing songs about nature.

Art

Stencils—Use the patterns as guides to cut nature shapes out of large pieces of posterboard or tag board to make stencils.

Necklaces—Use the patterns as guides to cut nature shapes out of construction paper. Let the children each decorate one or more shapes. Have the children string their shapes on pieces of yarn.

Stamps—Use the patterns as guides to cut nature shapes out of sponges. Glue the sponge shapes to blocks of wood to make stamps.

Classroom Aids

Room Decorations—Use the patterns as guides to cut out nature shapes for decorating bulletin boards or creating a frieze.

Calendar Markers—Use one of the smaller patterns as a guide to cut nature shapes, one for each day of the month, out of construction paper. Number the shapes and arrange them in a calendar format on a bulletin board.

Name Tags—Use the patterns as guides to cut nature shapes out of construction paper. Write a child's name on each shape and string it on a piece of yarn.

Learning Games

Matching—Use the patterns as guides to cut various sizes and kinds of nature shapes out of various colors of construction paper or felt. Let the children match the shapes by size, kind, or color.

Counting—Use the patterns as guides to cut various sizes and kinds of nature shapes out of various colors of construction paper or felt. Ask the children to count the large shapes, the red shapes or all of the tulip shapes.

Sizing—Use the patterns as guides to cut four sizes of one object's shape out of construction paper or felt. Have the children arrange the shapes by size.

Sorting—Use the patterns as guides to cut various sizes and kinds of nature shapes out of various colors of construction paper or felt. Let the children sort the shapes by size, kind, color or type.

Card Games—Photocopy and cut out the game cards. Cover them with clear self-stick paper. Help the children use the cards to play such games as Go Fish, Concentration, Lotto and Bingo.

Daisy 11

Rose 15

Tulip 19

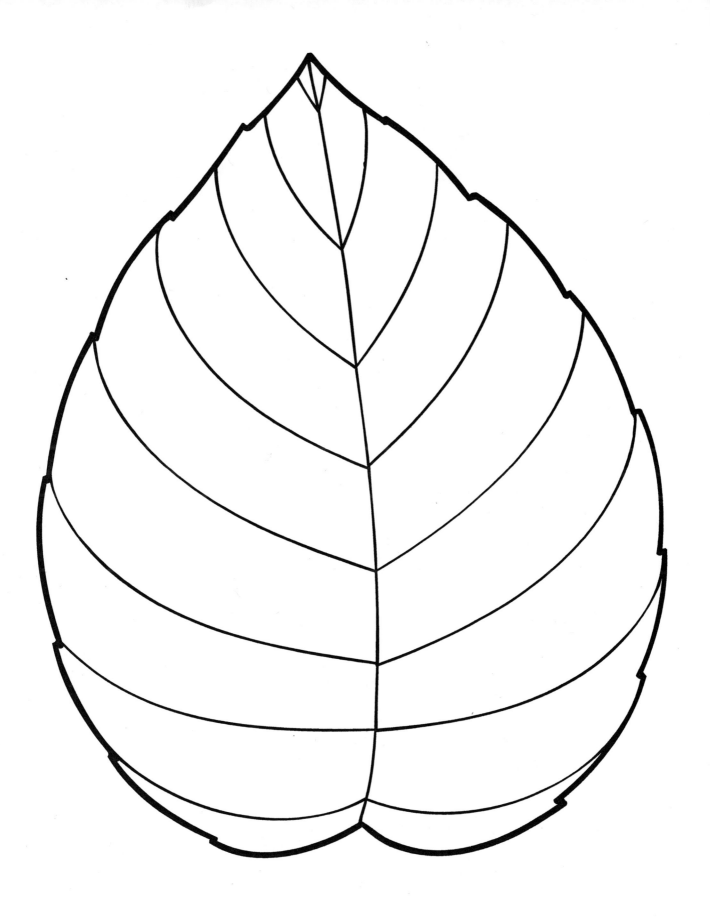

Birch Leaf 27

Birch Leaf 29

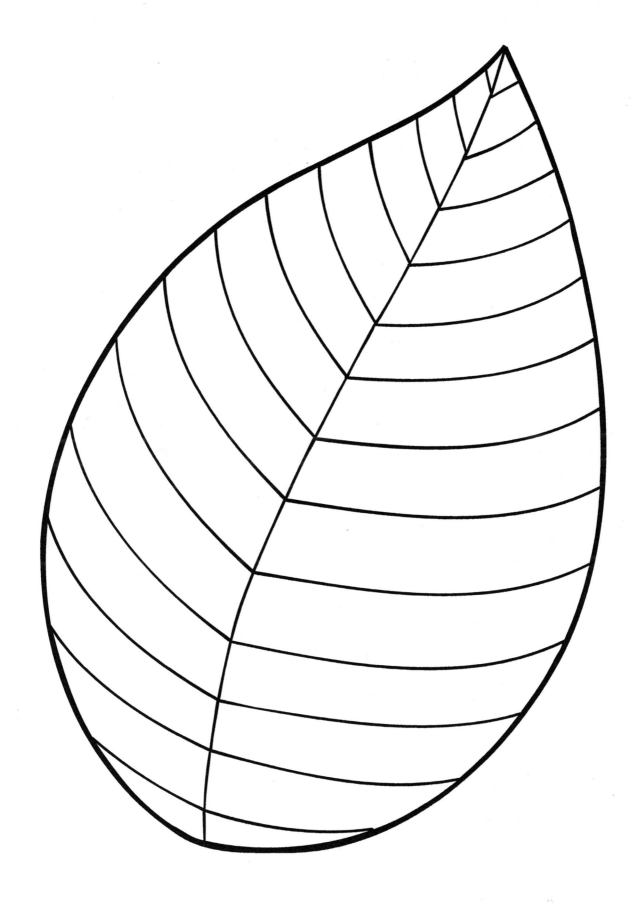

Elm Leaf 31

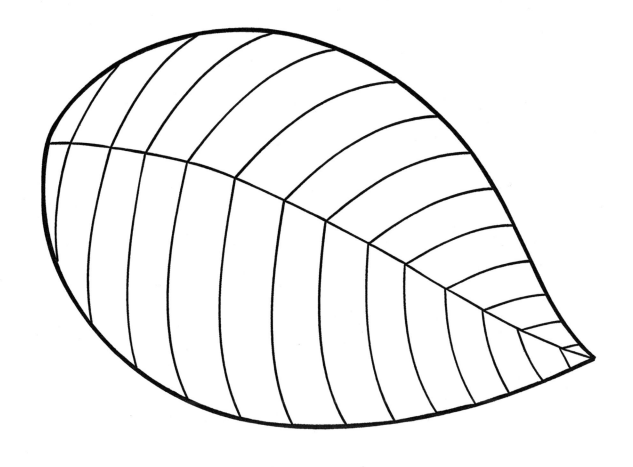

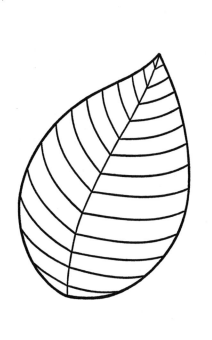

Elm Leaf 33

Ivy Leaf 35

Maple Leaf 39

Maple Leaf 41

Oak Leaf 43

Oak Leaf 45

Bush 47

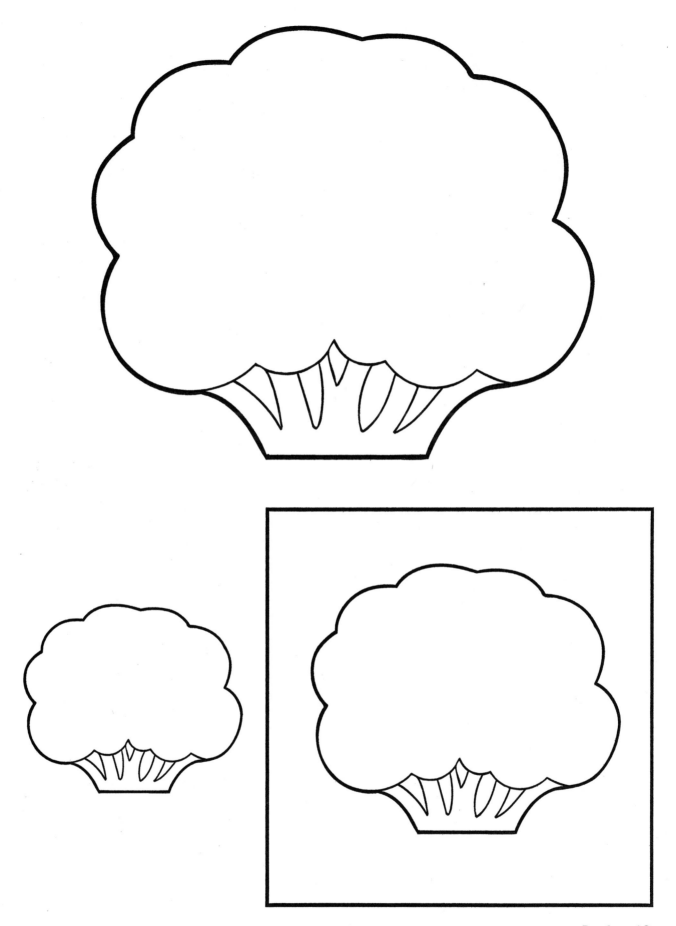

Bush 49

Evergreen Tree 53

Fruit Tree 55

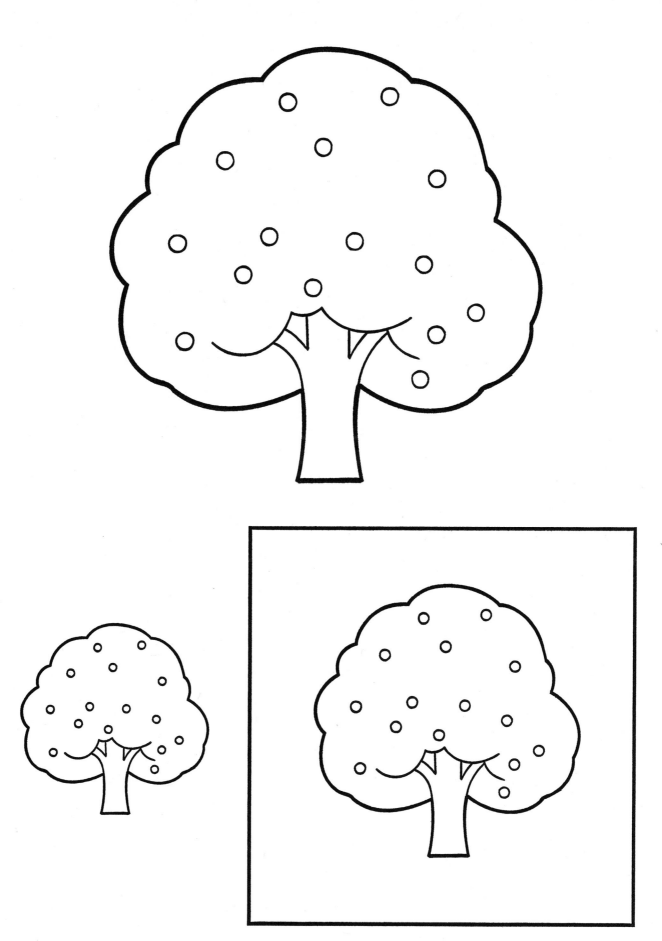

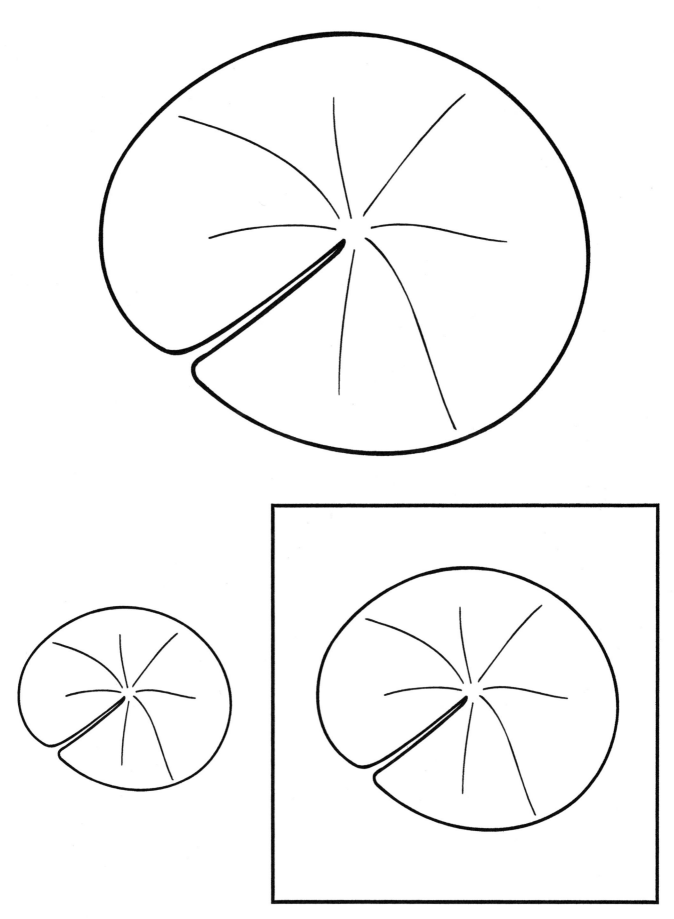

Lily Pad 61

Palm Tree 63

Pine Cone 67

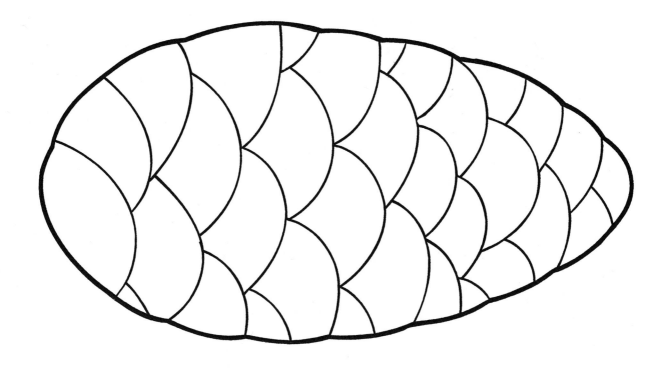

Pine Cone 69

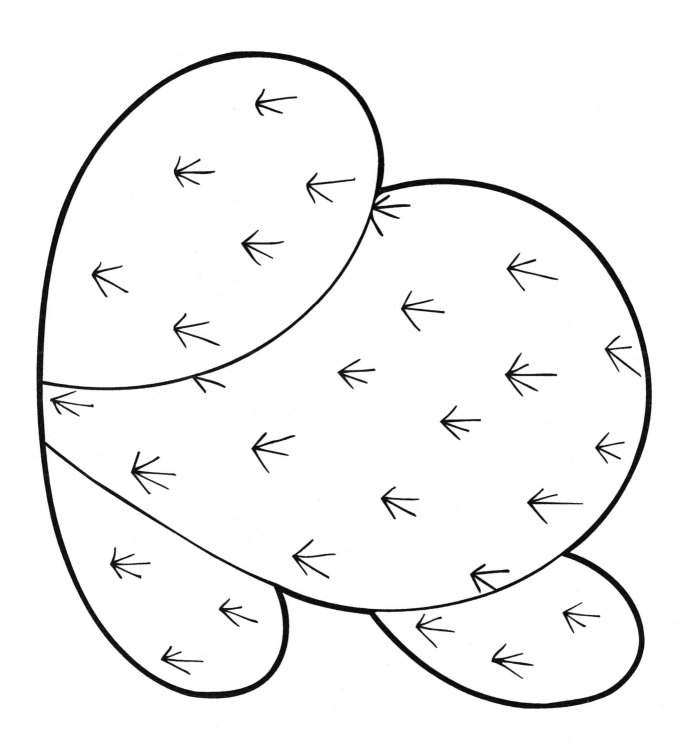

Prickly Pear Cactus 71

Prickly Pear Cactus 73

Saguaro Cactus 75

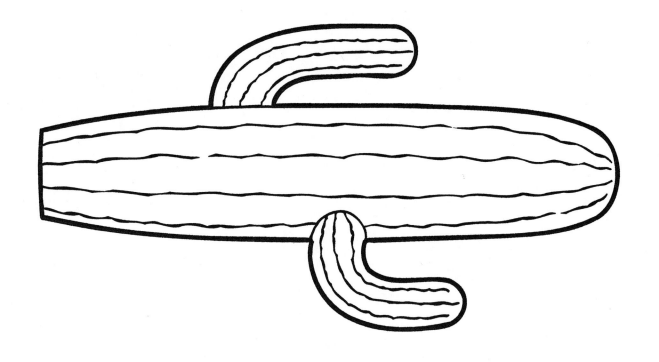

Saguaro Cactus 77

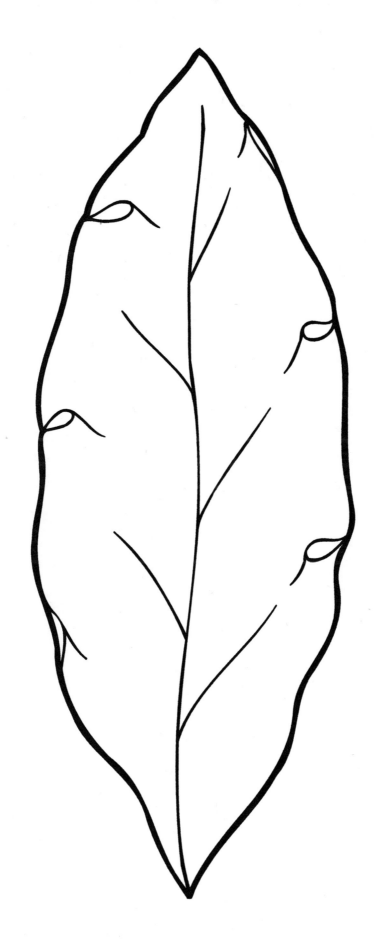

Seaweed 79

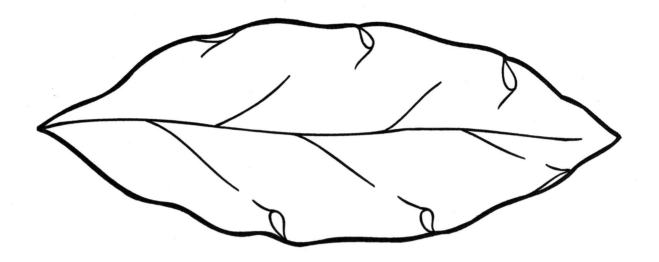

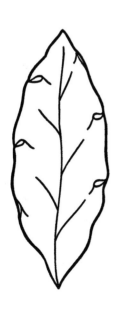

Cloud 83

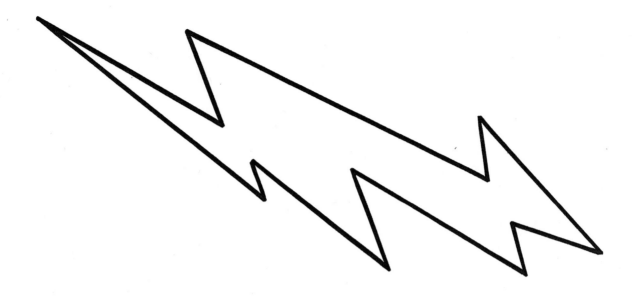

Lightning 89

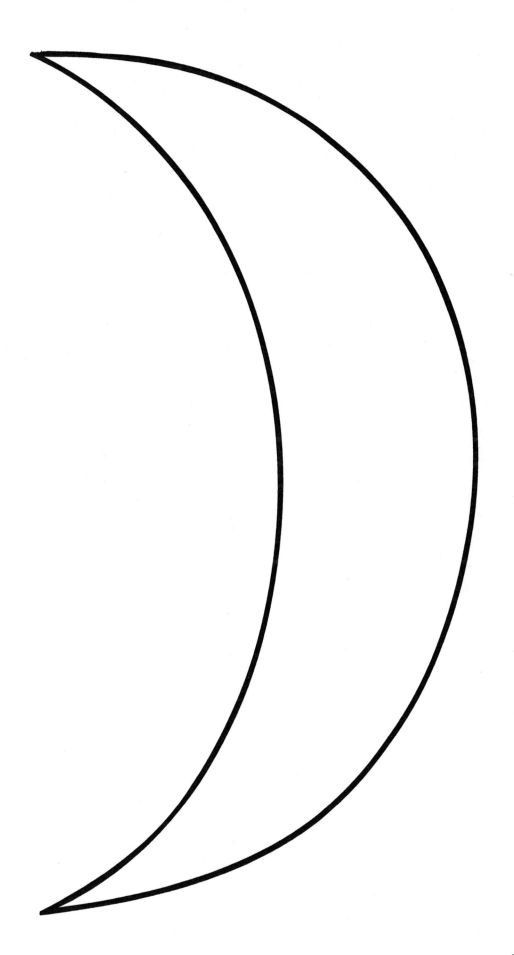

Moon 91

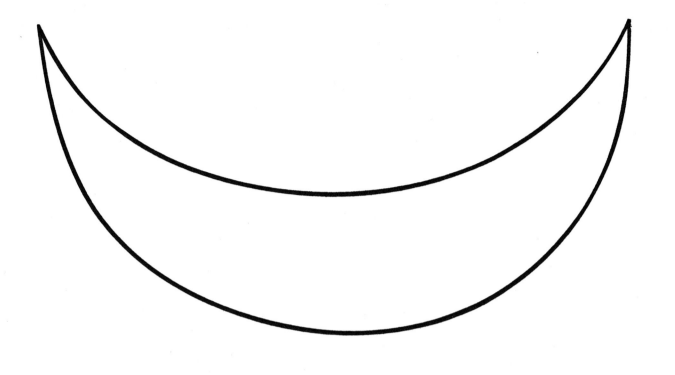

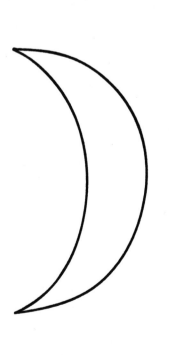

Moon 93

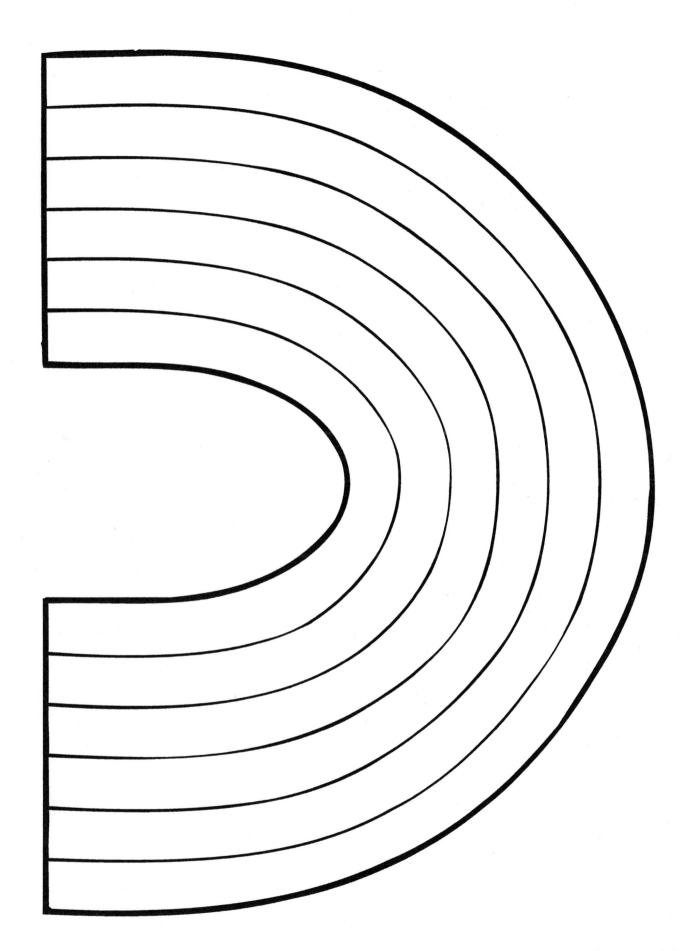

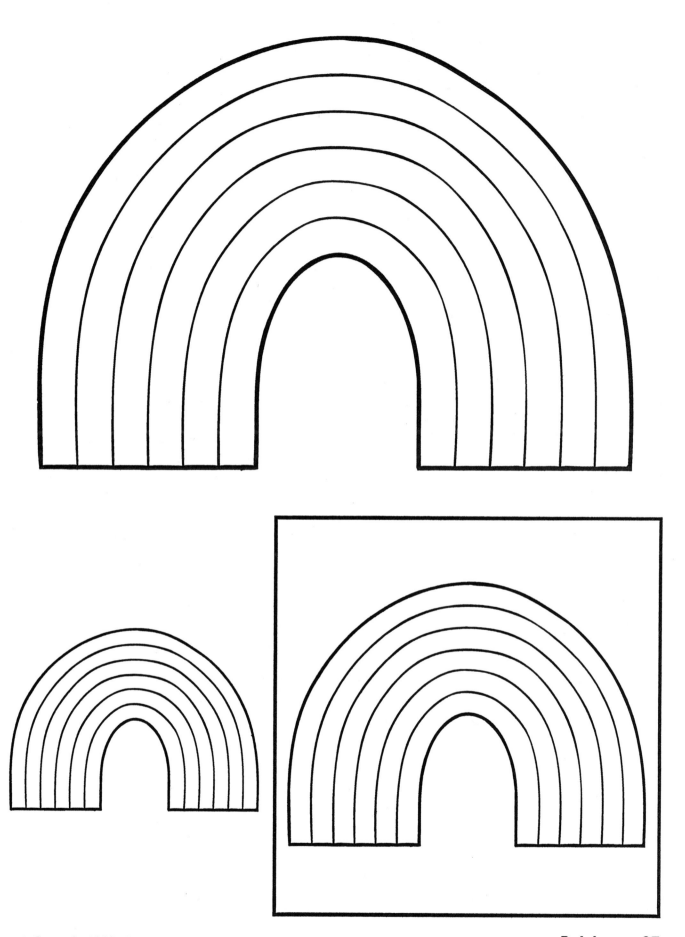

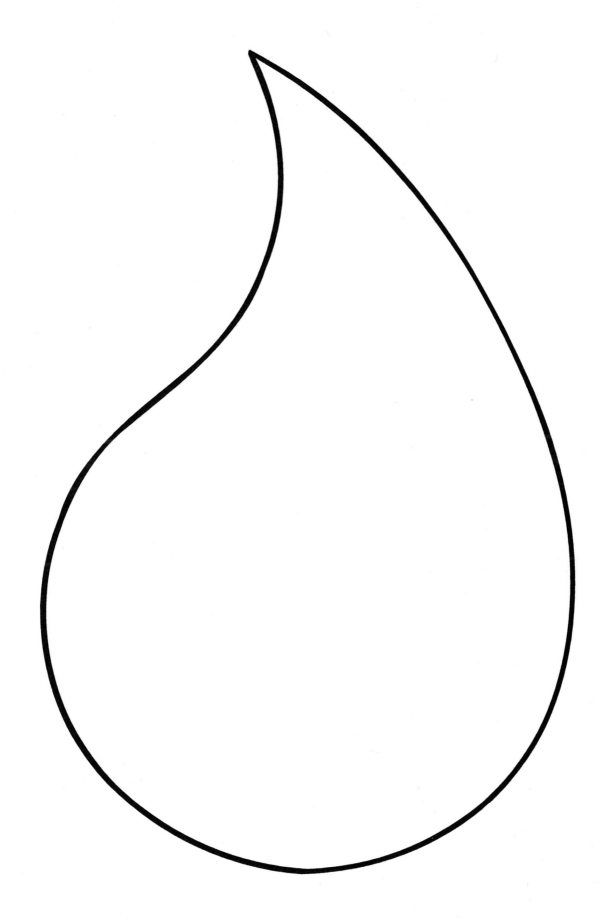

Raindrop   99

Raindrop 101

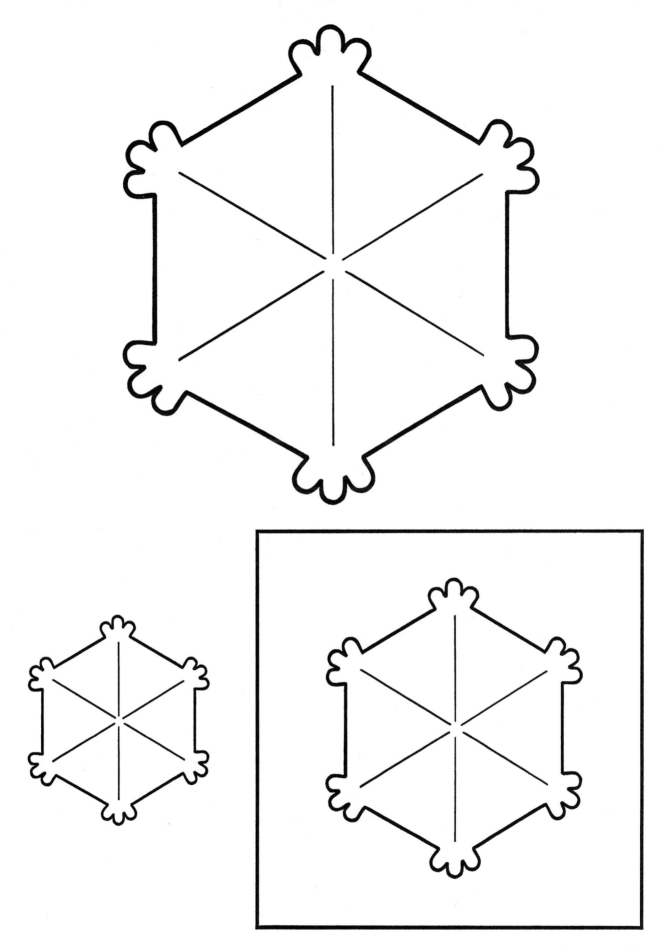

Snowflake 105

Sun 109

Wind 111

Wind 113

Bread 115

Bread 117

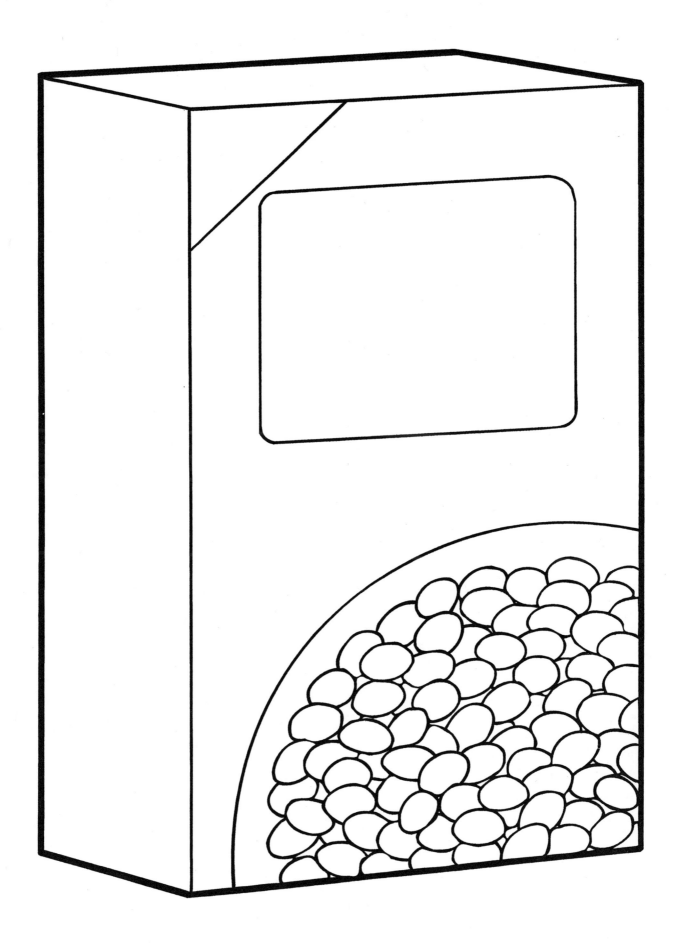

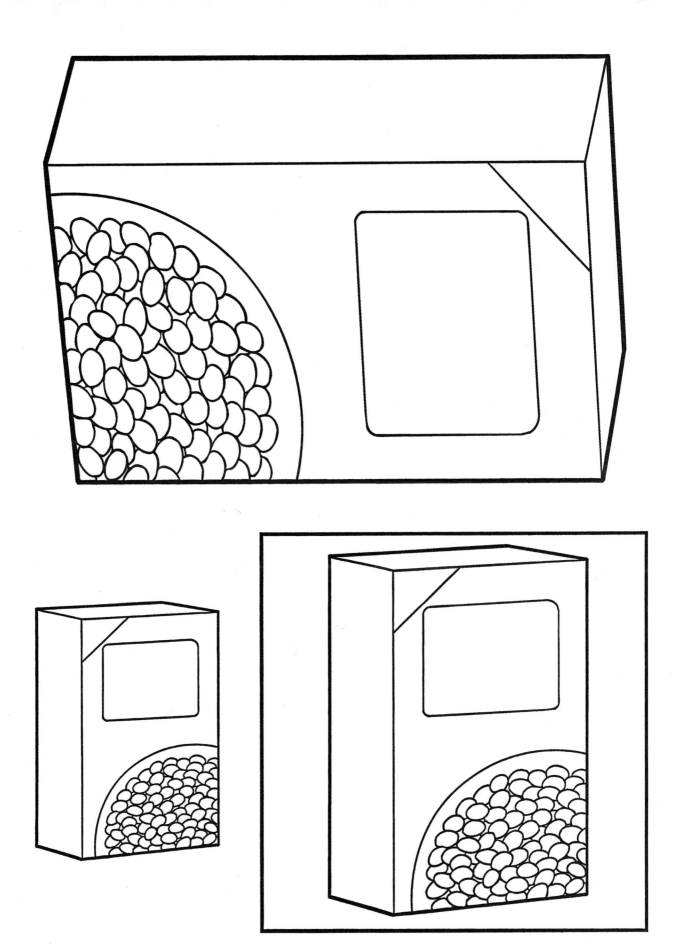

Cereal 121

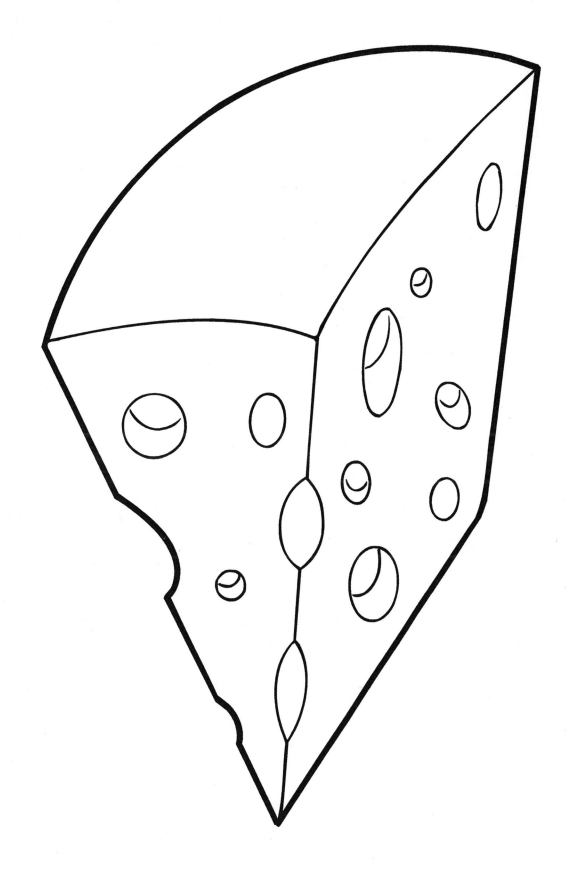

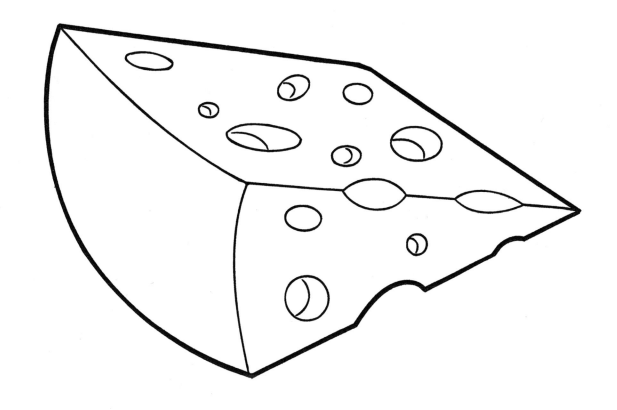

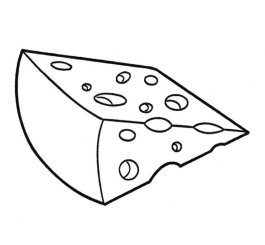

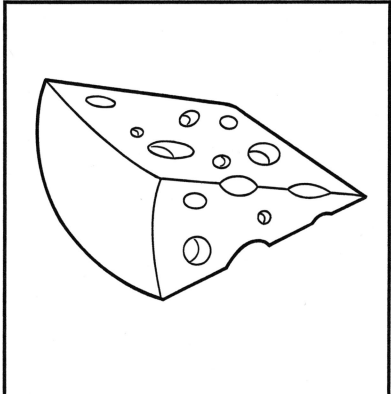

Cheese 125

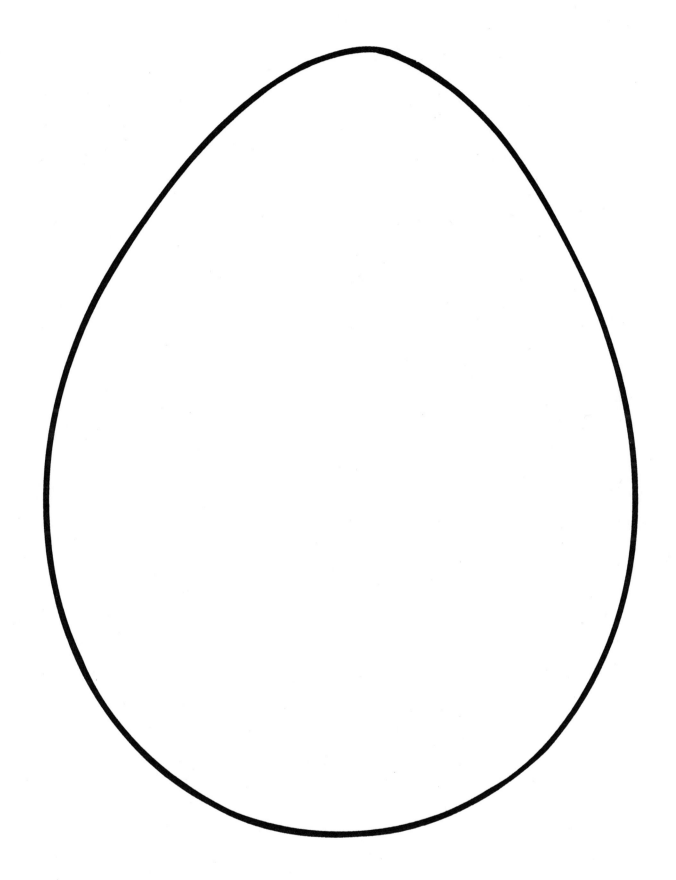

Egg 127

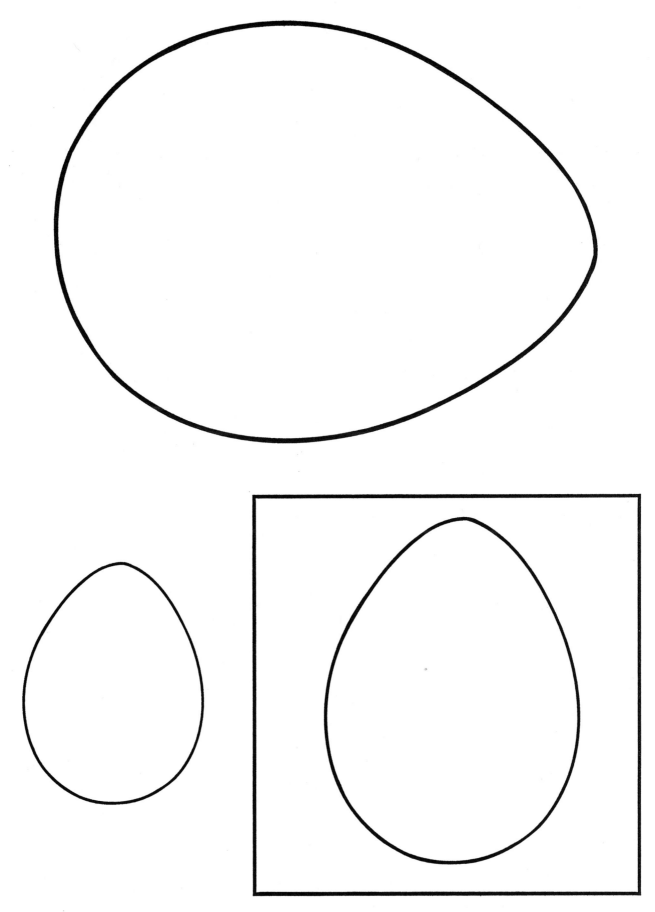

Egg 129

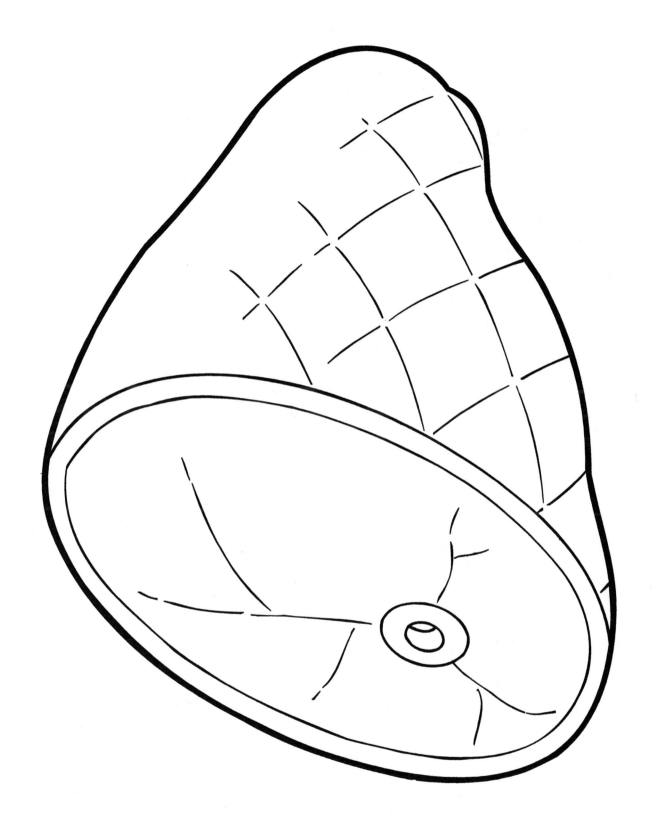

Ham 131

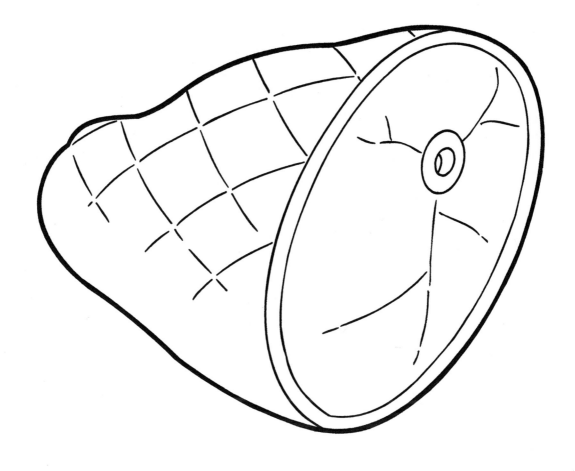

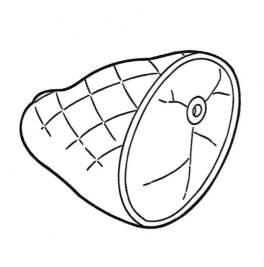

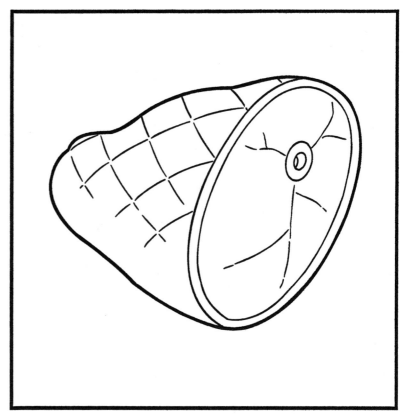

Ham 133

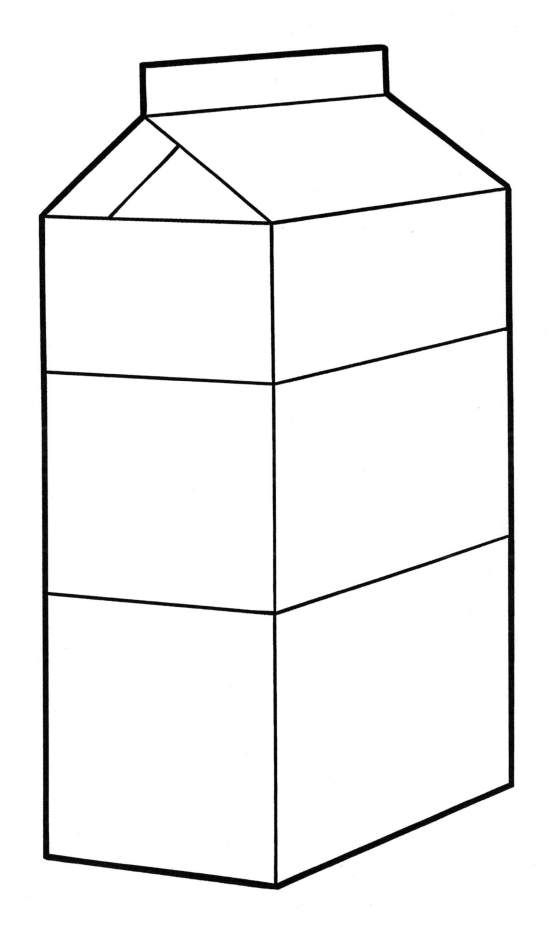

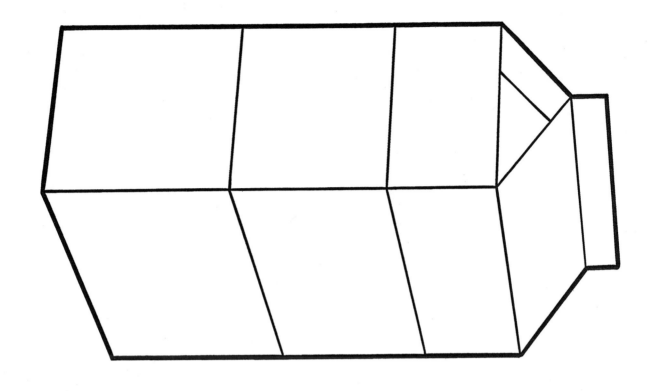

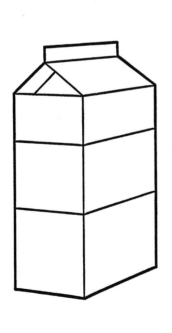

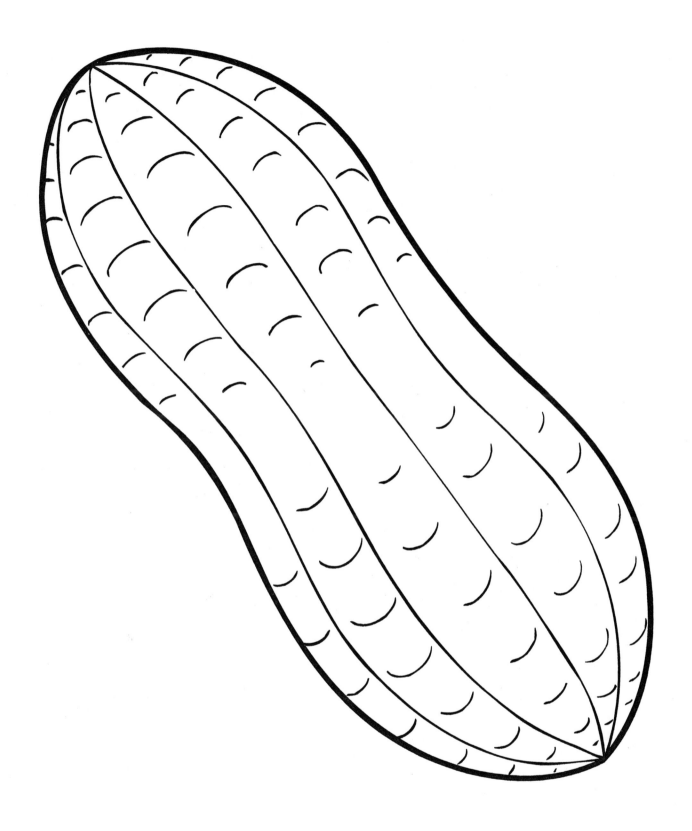

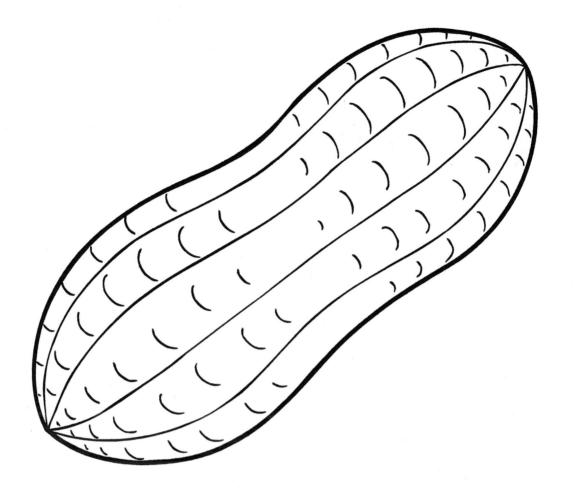

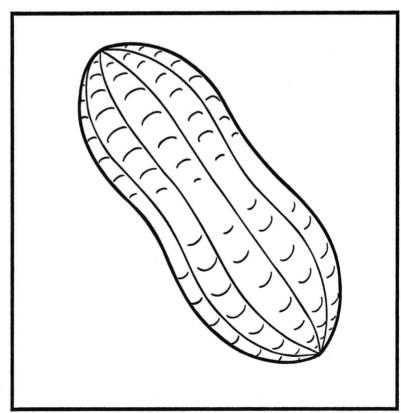

Peanut 141

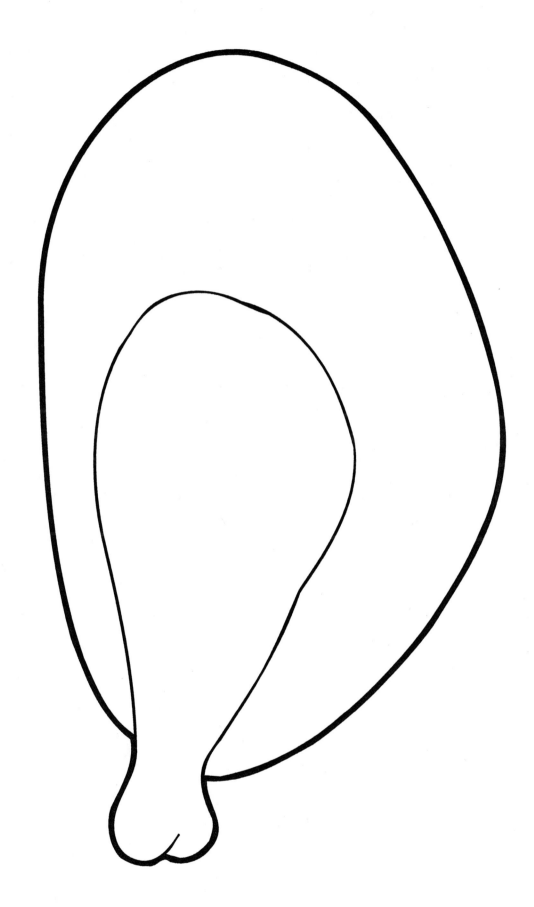

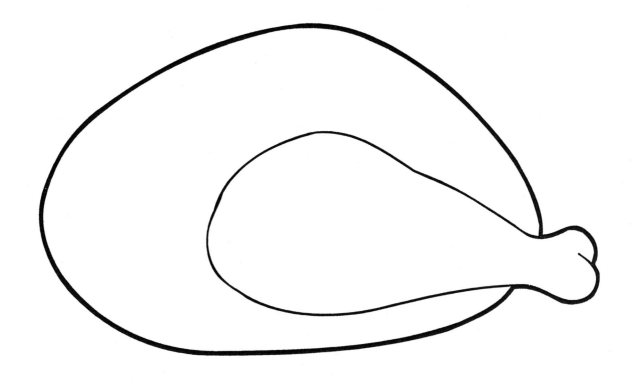

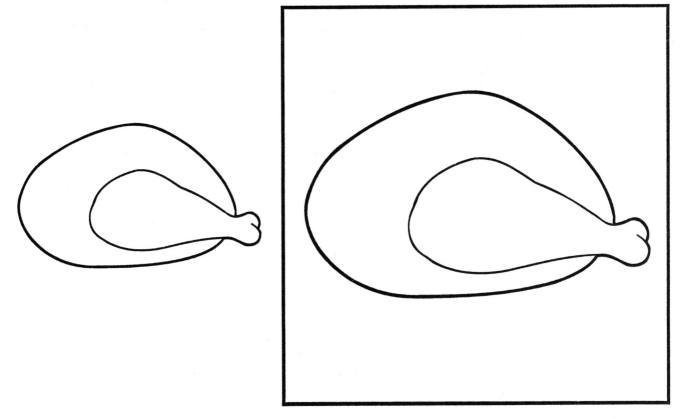

Roast Turkey 145

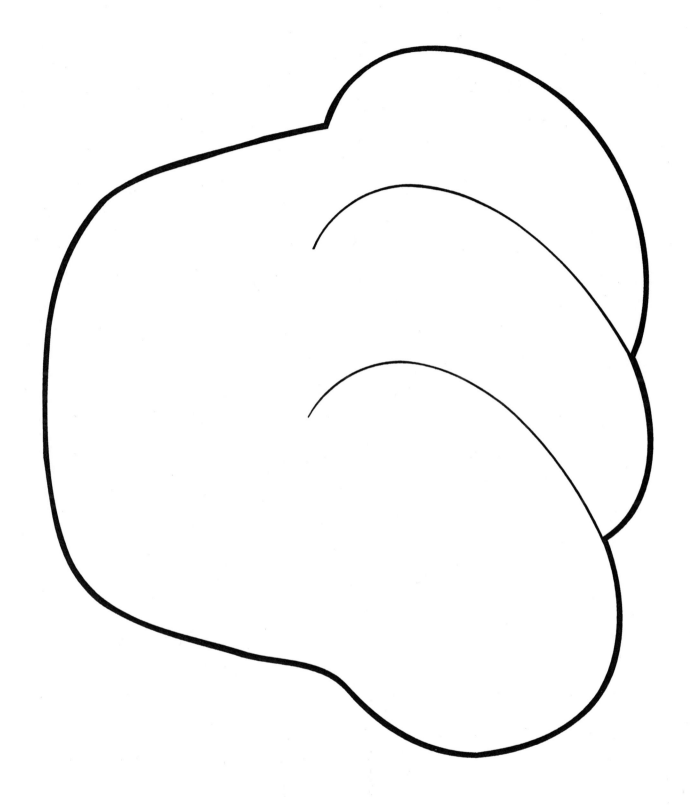

Roll   147

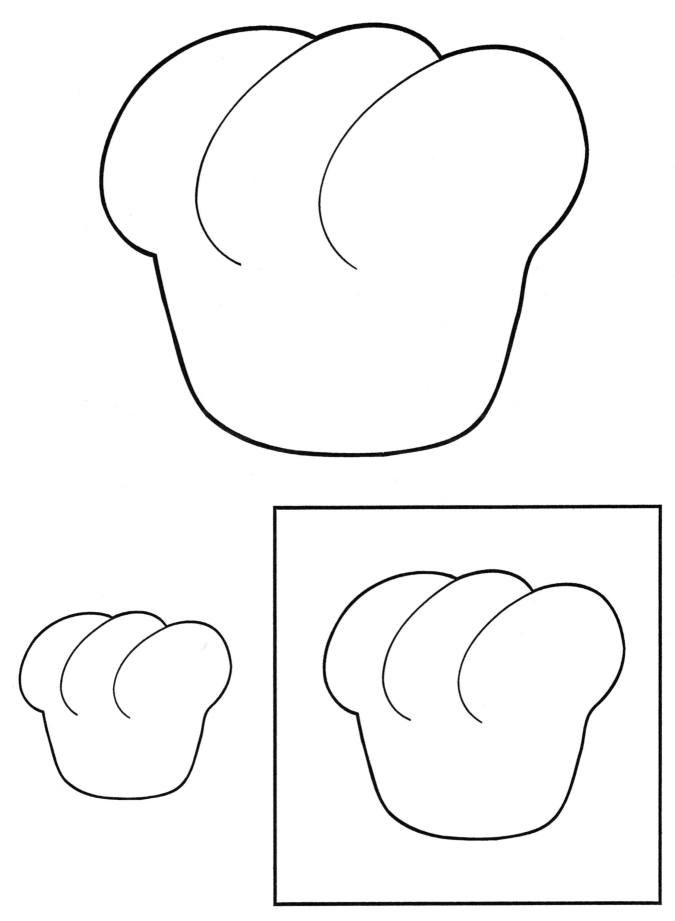

Roll 149

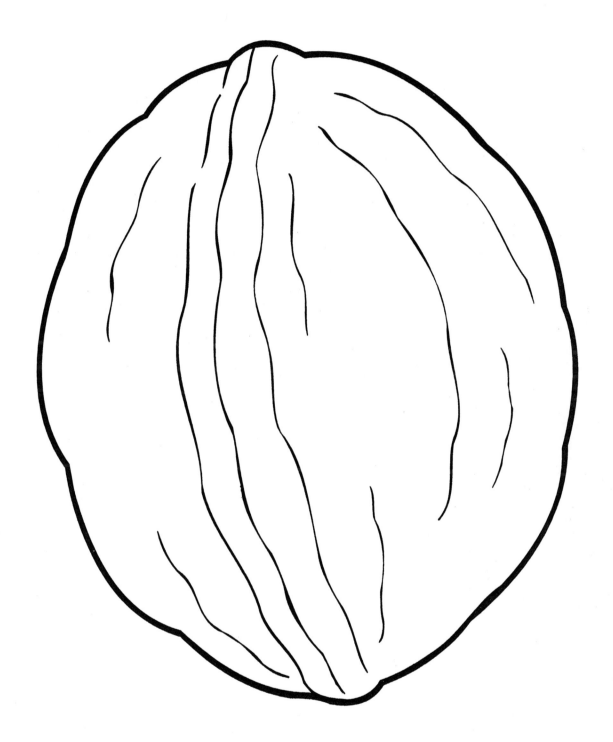

Walnut 151

Walnut 153

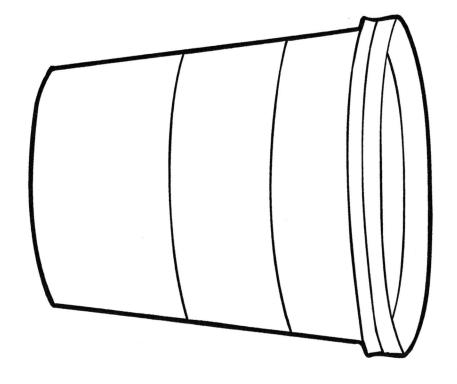

Apple 159

Apple 161

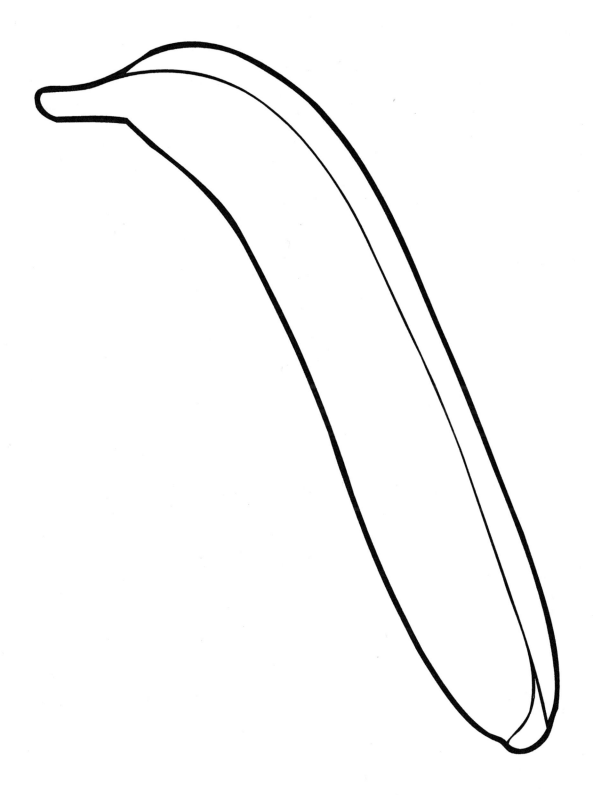

Banana 163

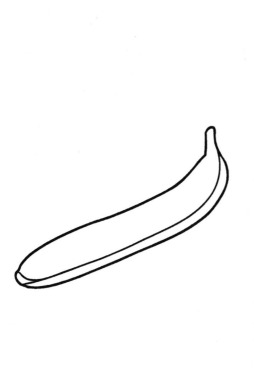

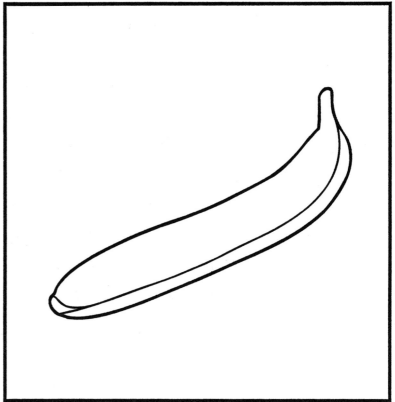

Banana 165

Cherries 167

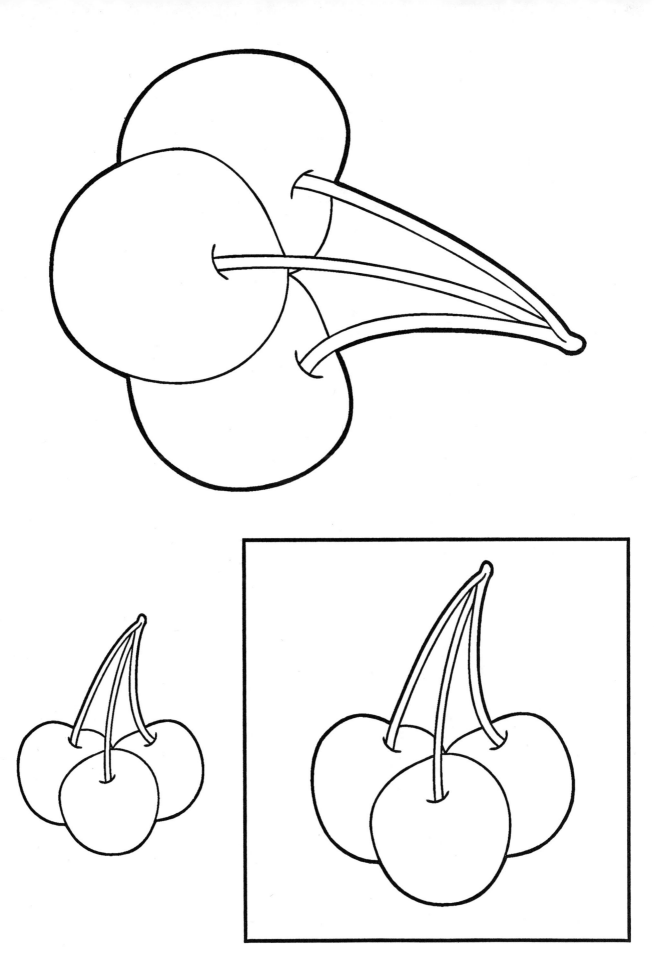

Cherries 169

Grapes 171

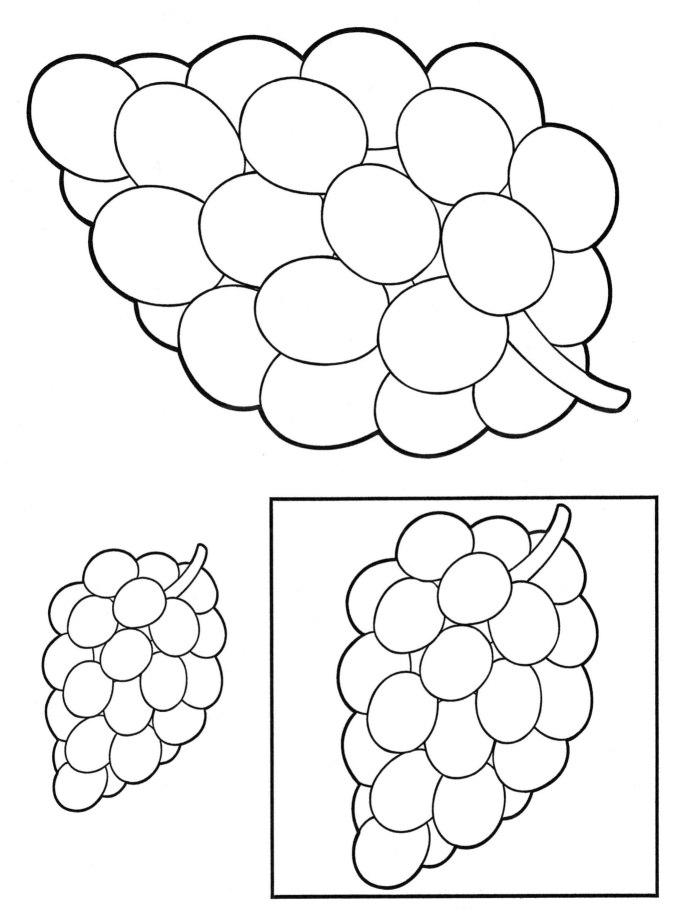

Grapes 173

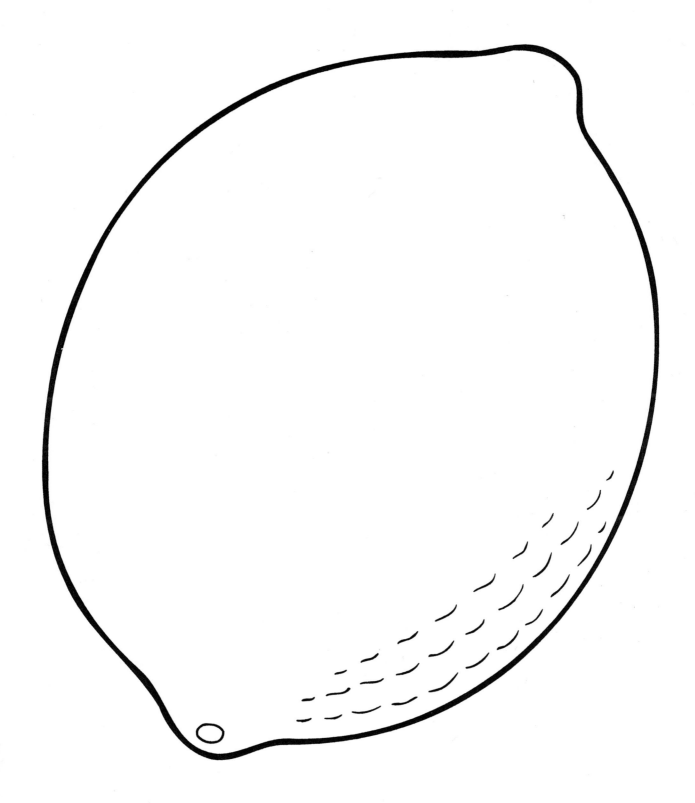

Lemon 175

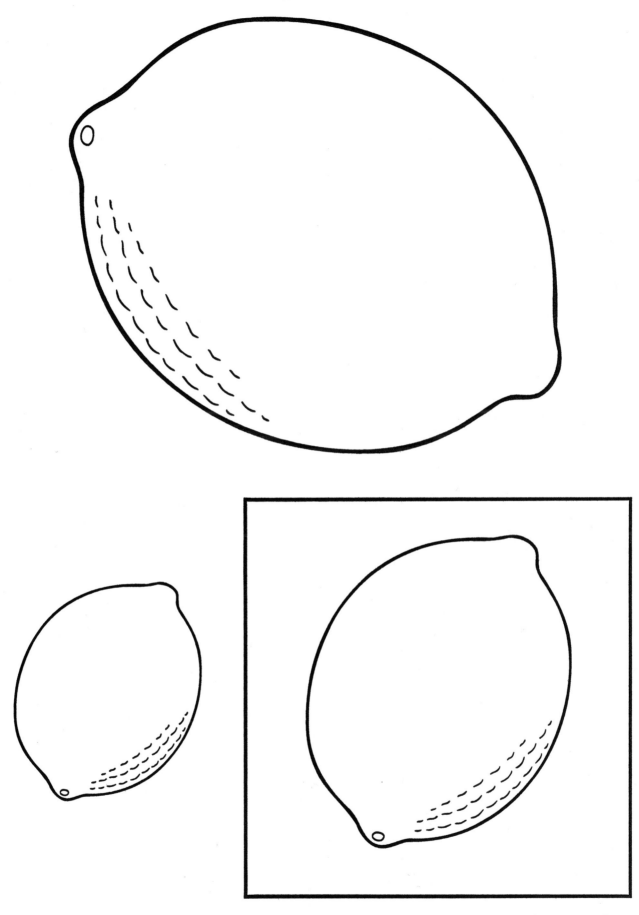

Lemon 177

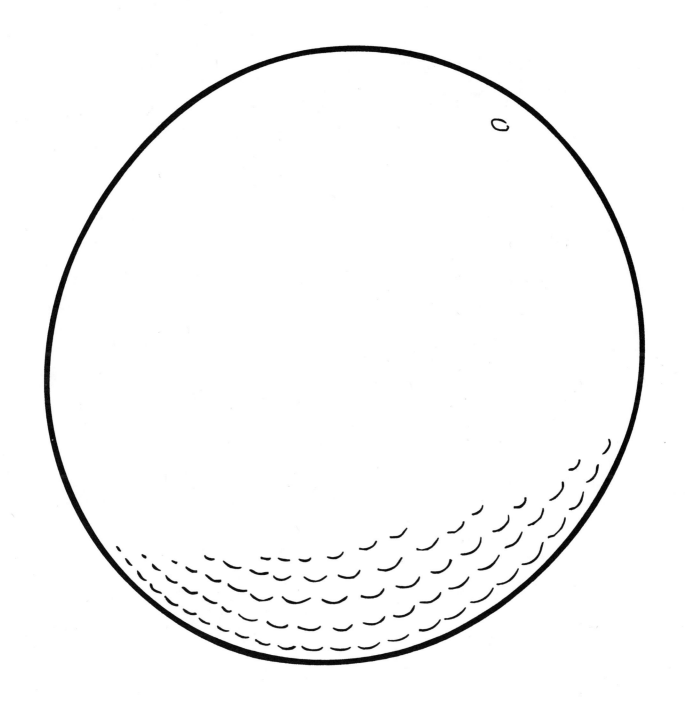

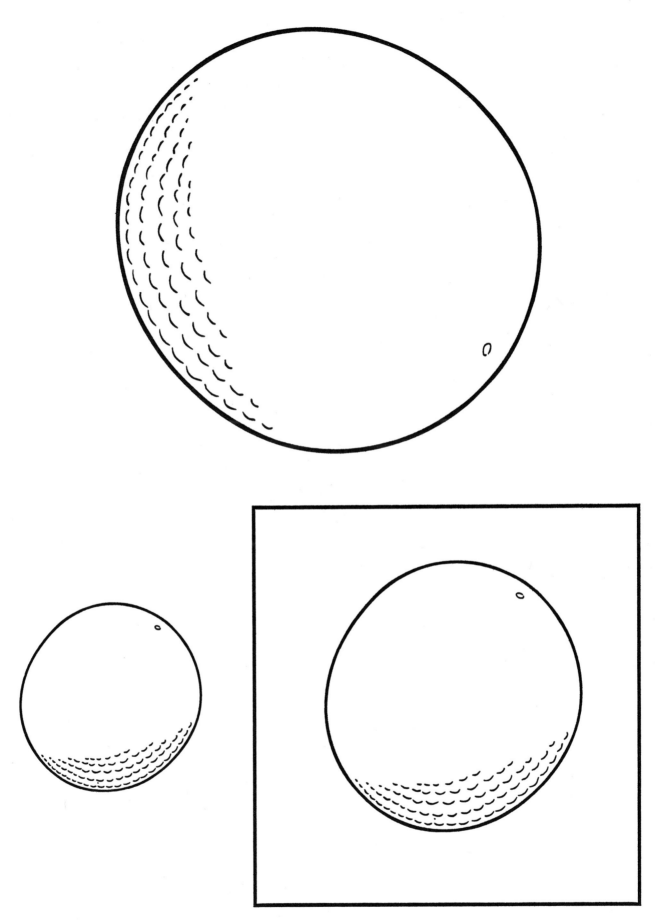

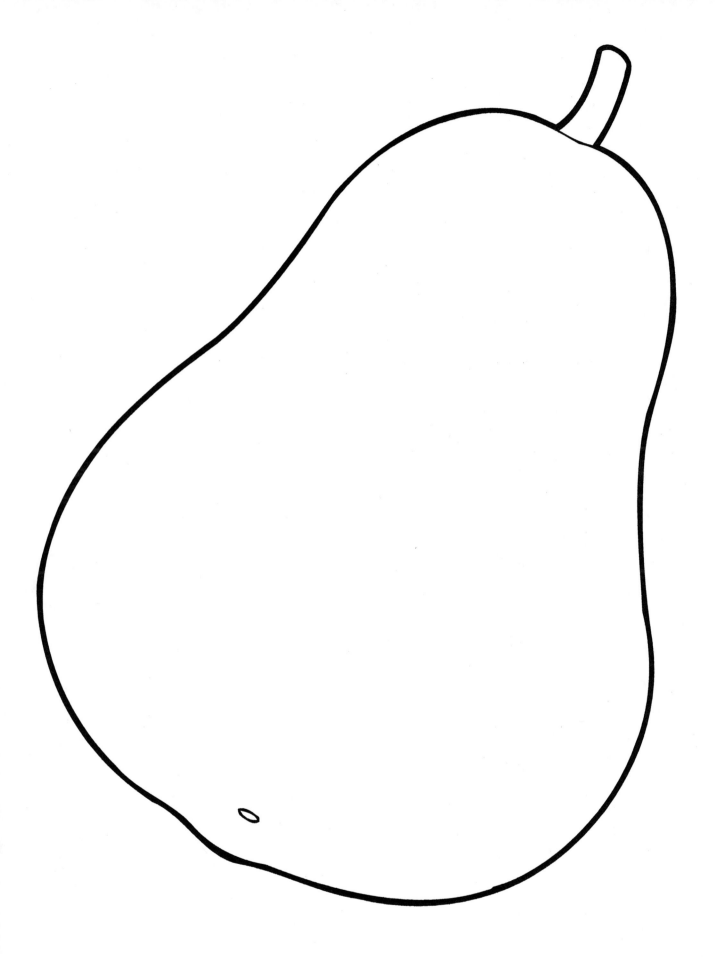

Pear 183

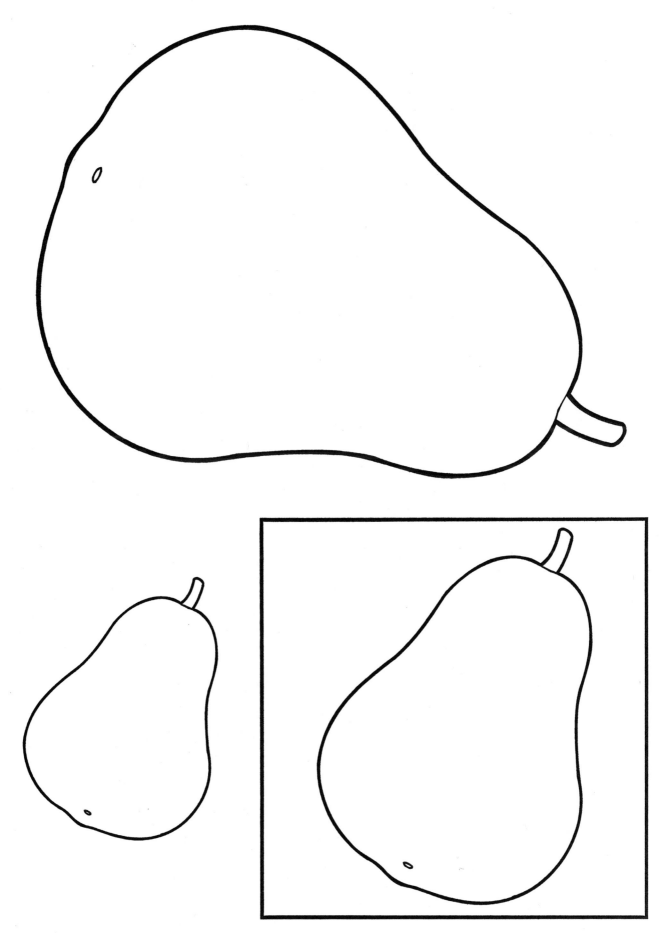

Pear 185

Pineapple 189

Strawberry 191

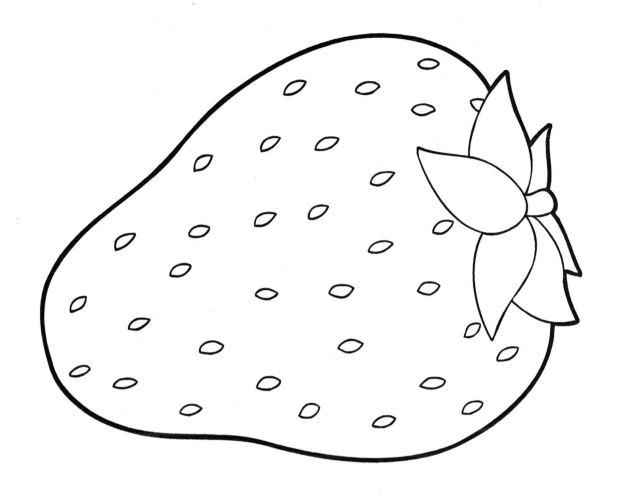

Strawberry 193

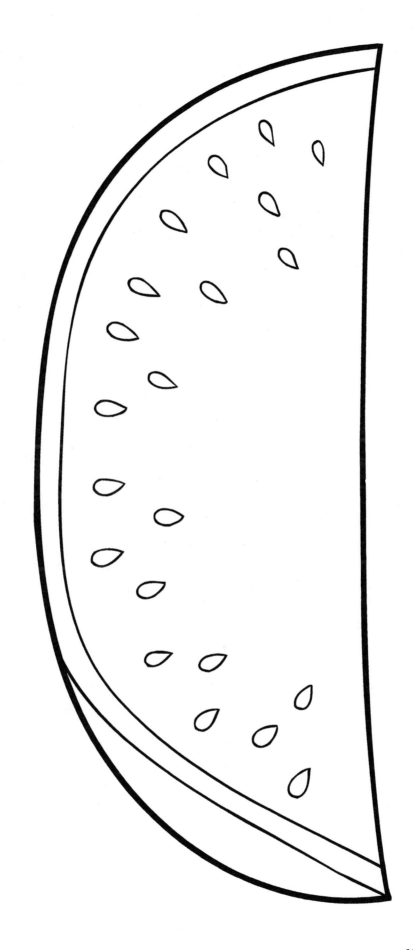

Watermelon 195

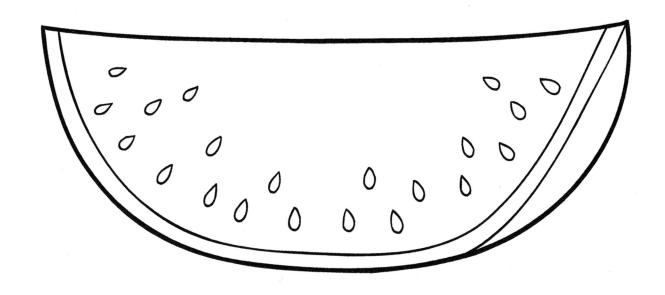

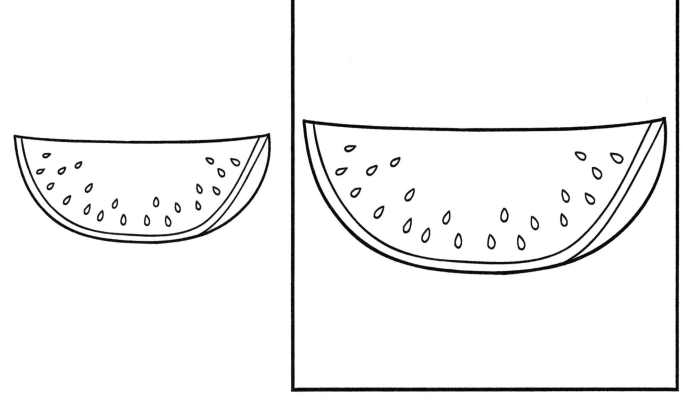

Watermelon 197

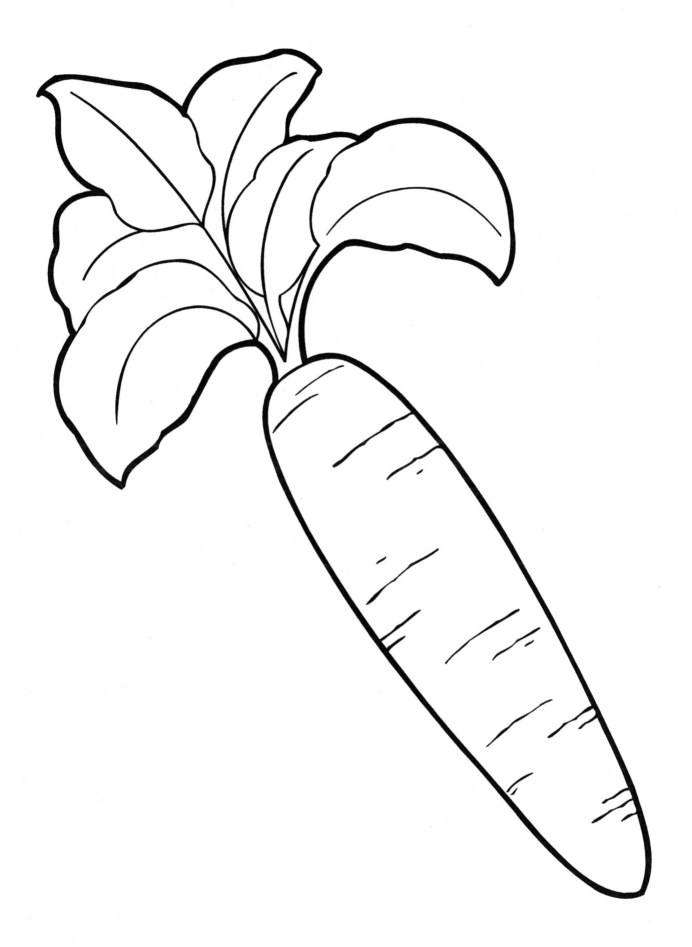

Carrot 199

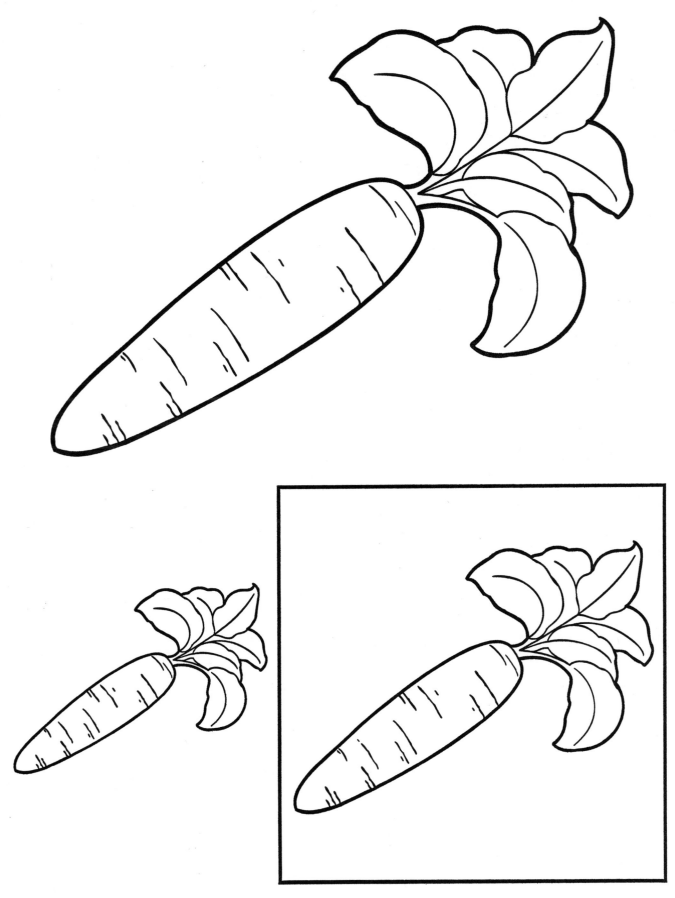

Carrot 201

Celery 203

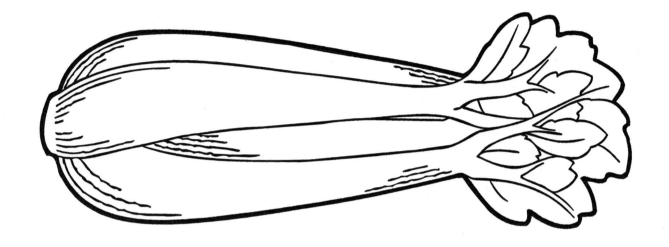

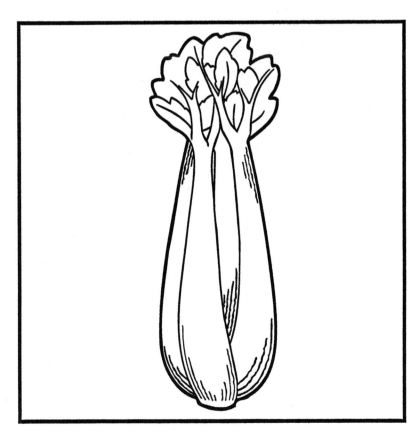

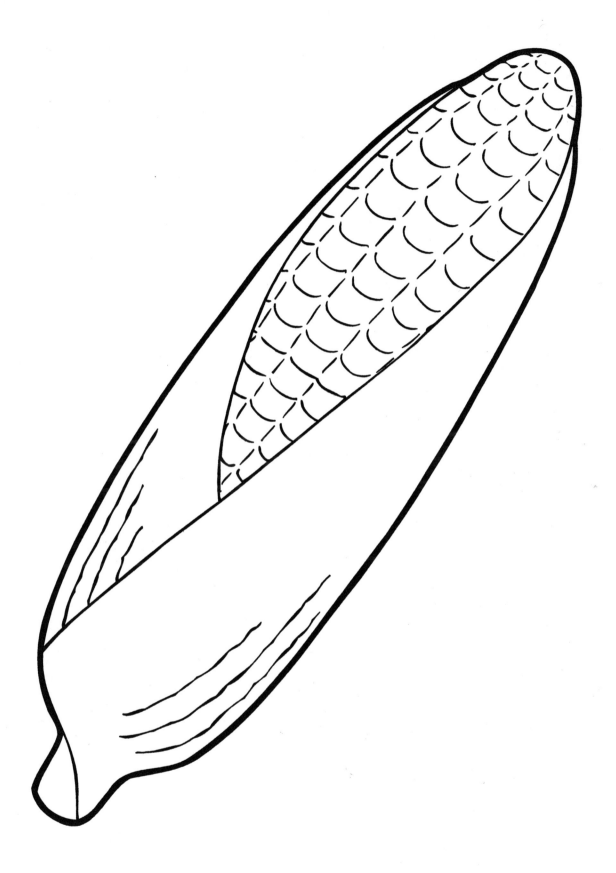

Corn 207

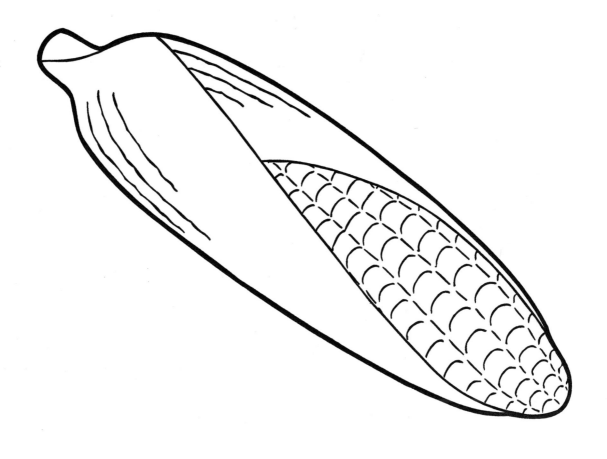

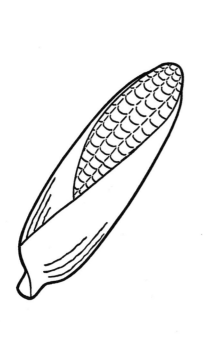

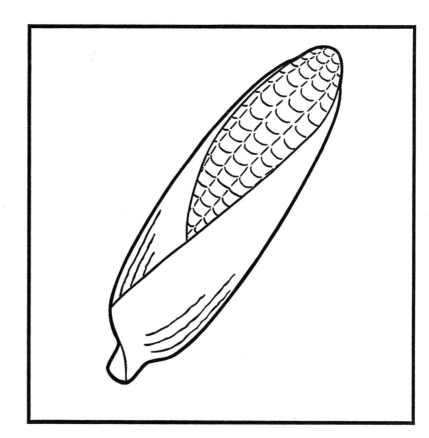

Corn 209

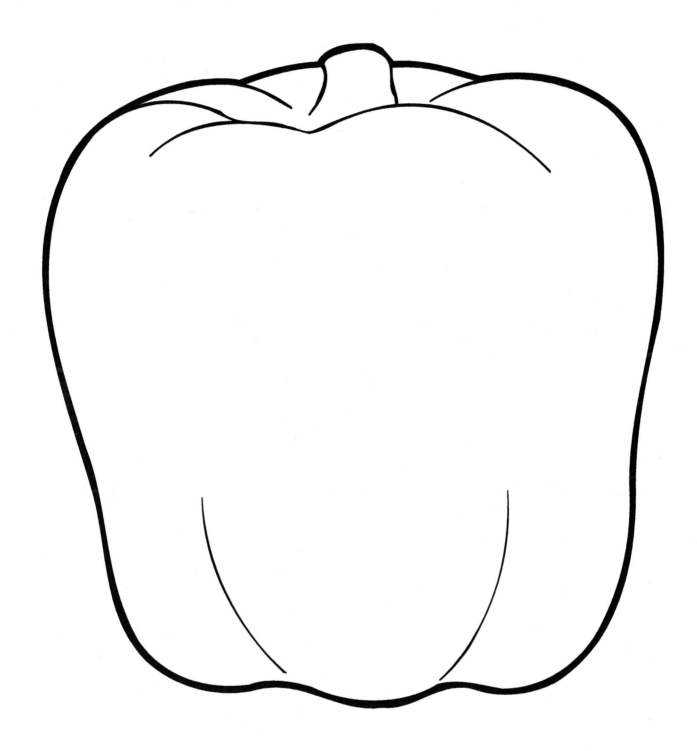

Green Pepper   211

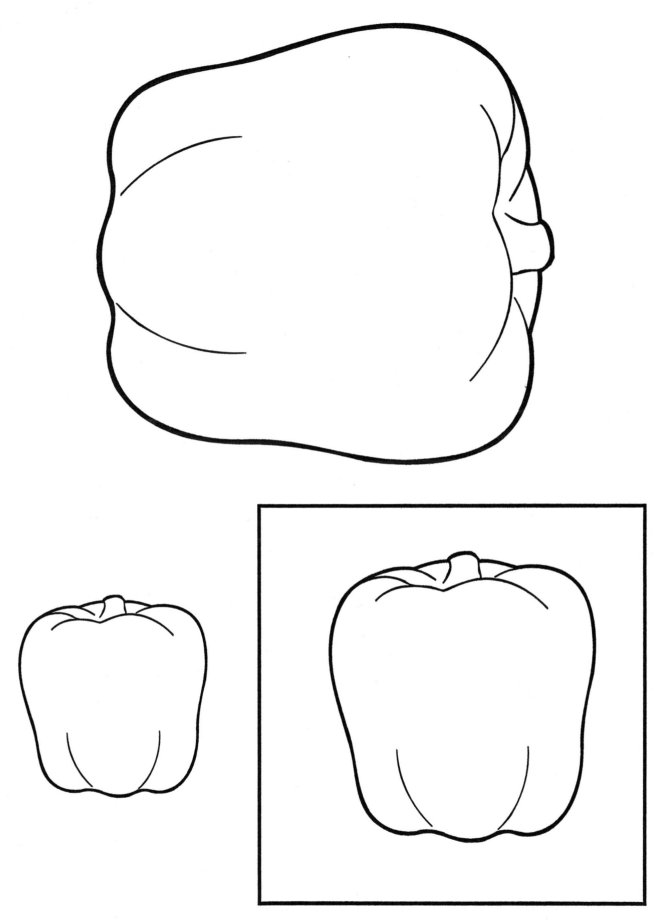

Green Pepper 213

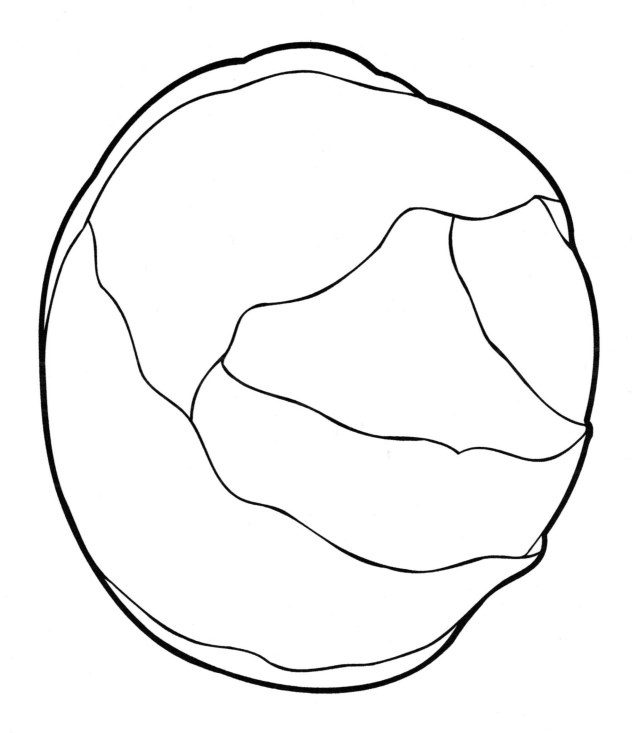

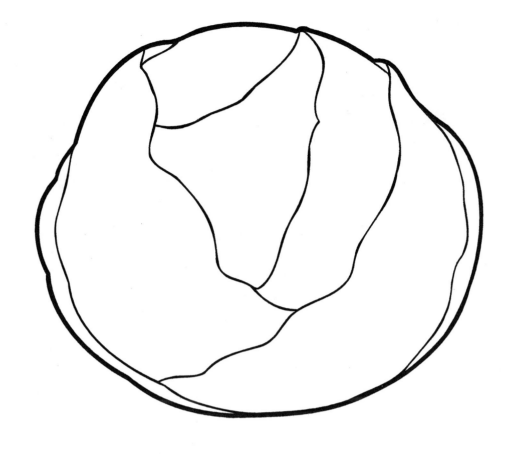

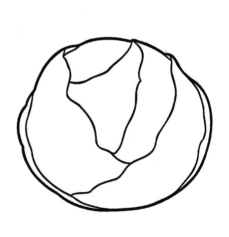

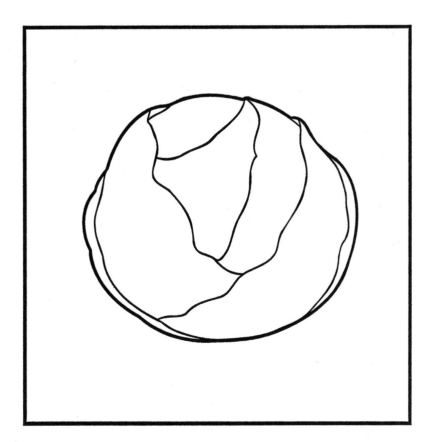

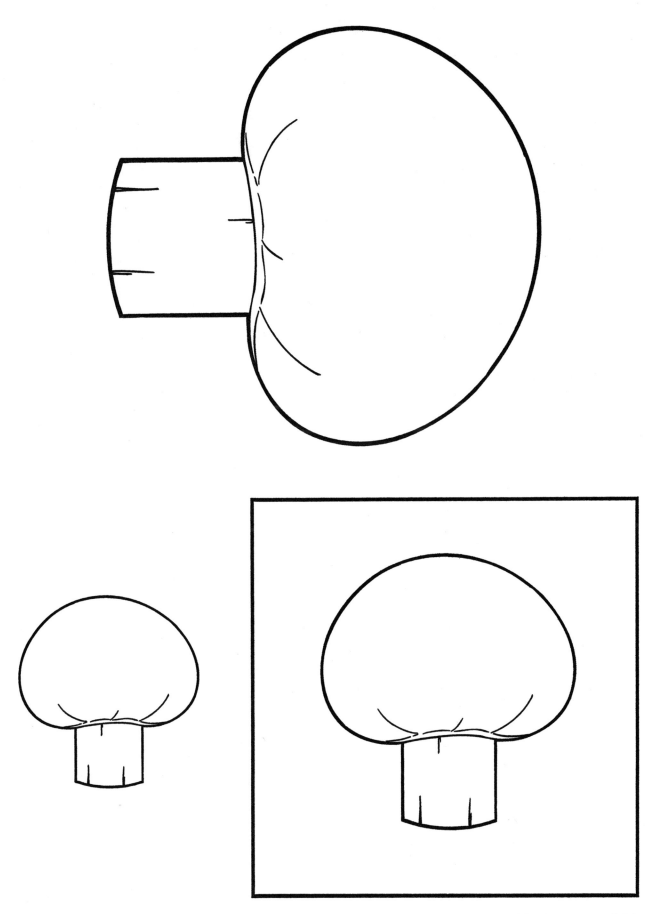

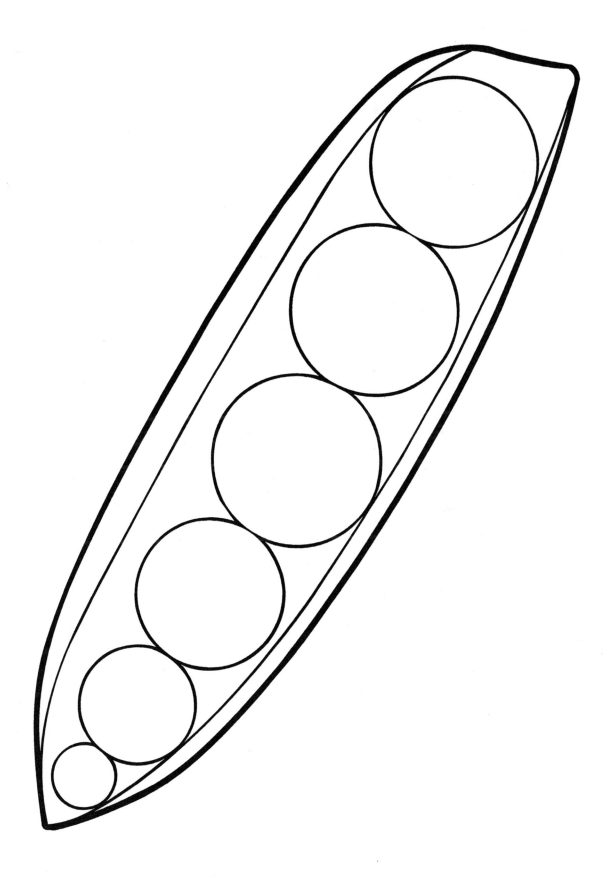

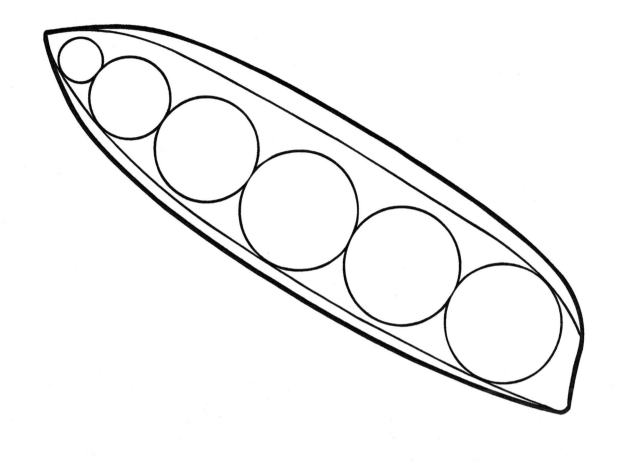

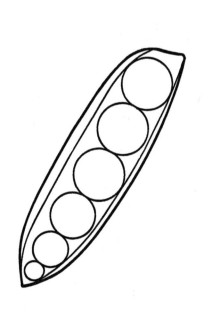

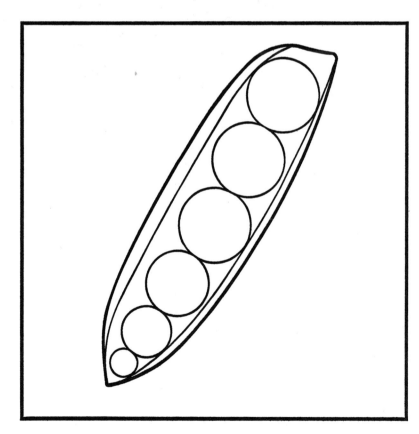

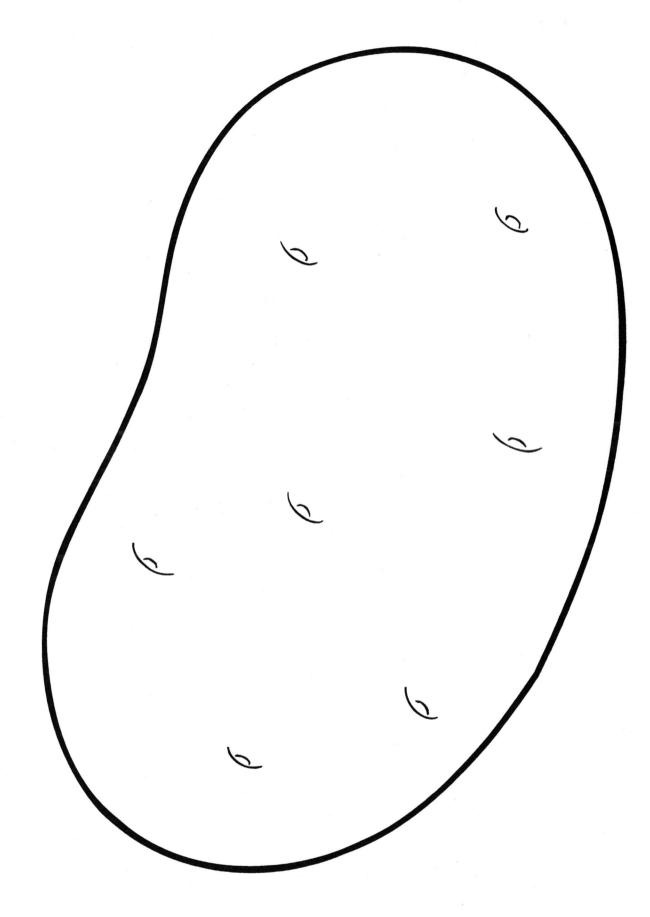

Potato 227

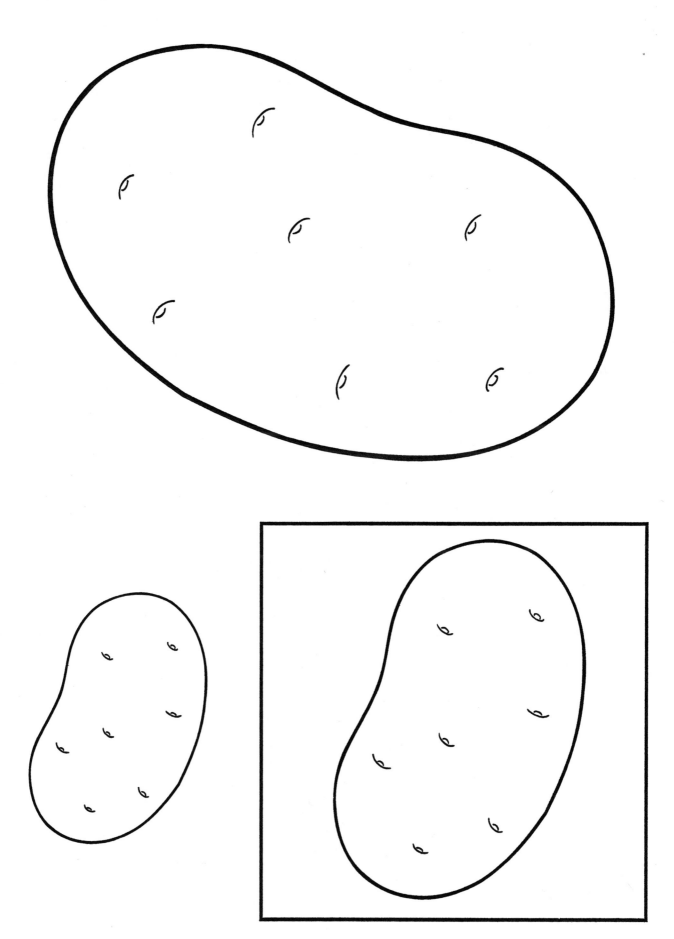

Potato 229

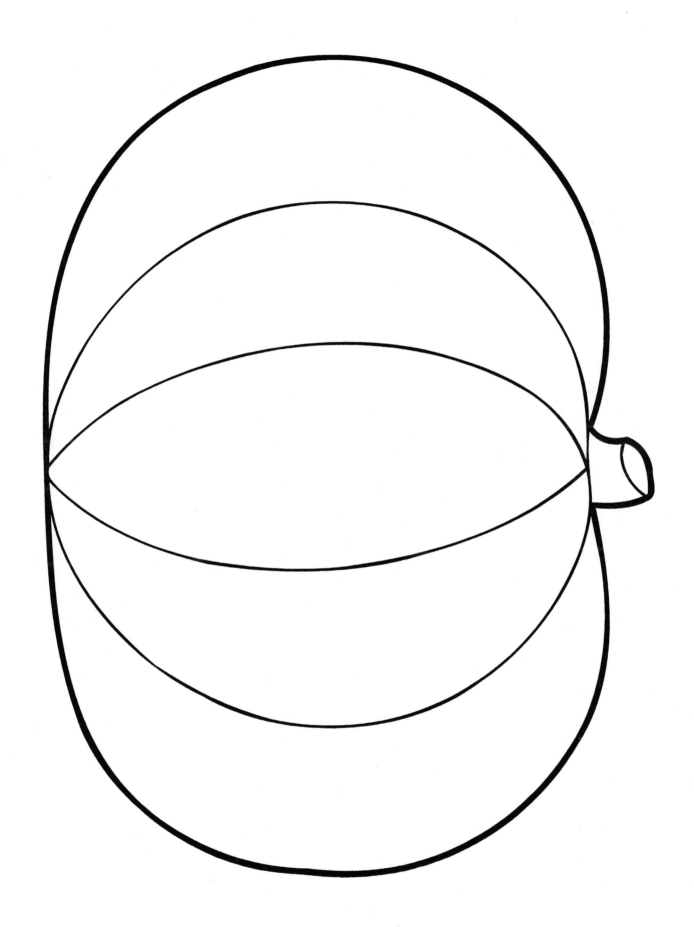

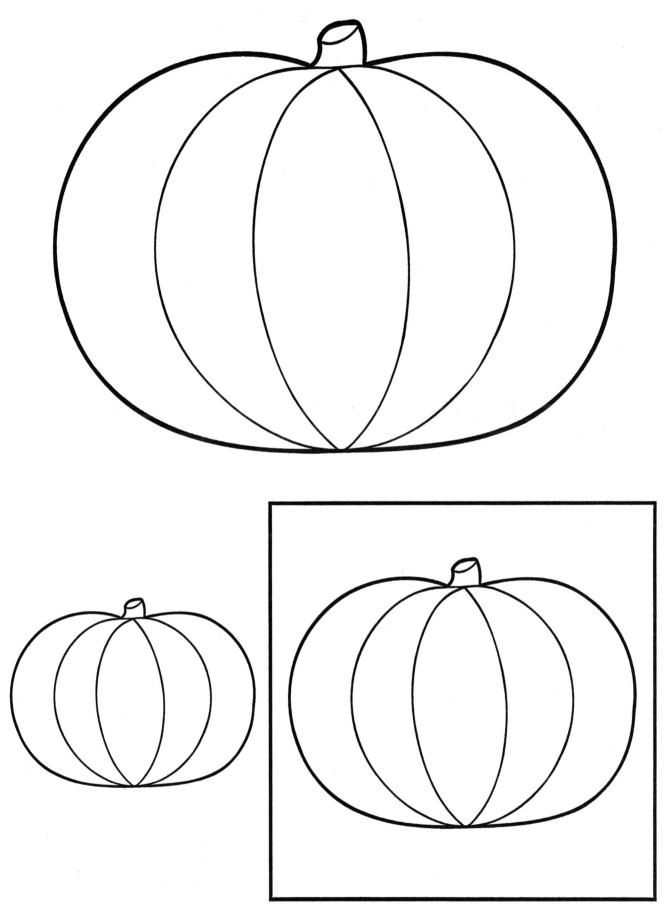

Pumpkin 233

Tomato 235

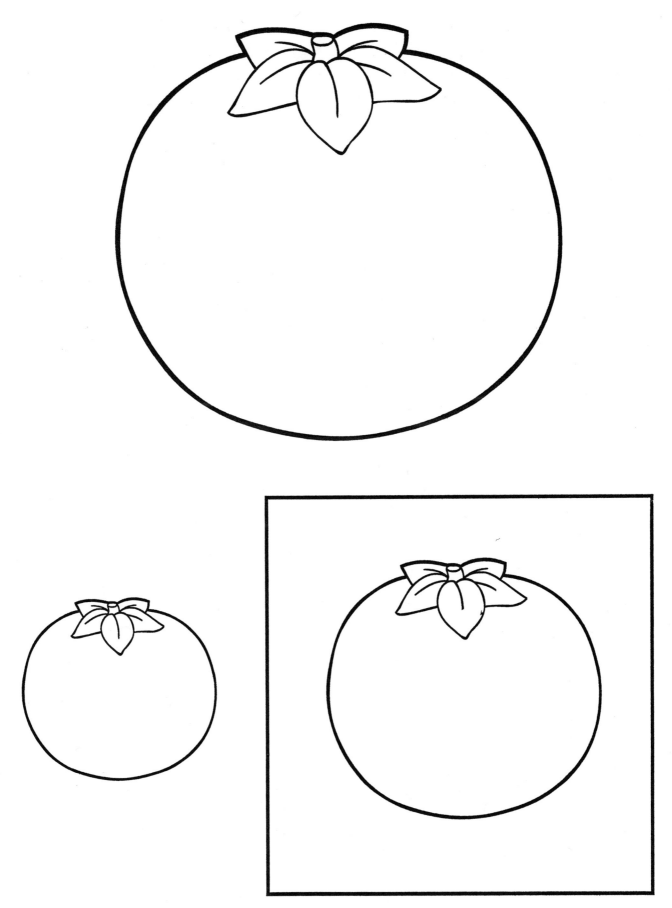

Tomato 237

INDEX

Totline Books

Super Snacks - 120 seasonal sugarless snack recipes kids love.

Teaching Tips - 300 helpful hints for working with young children.

Teaching Toys - over 100 toy and game ideas for teaching learning concepts.

Piggyback Songs - 110 original songs, sung to the tunes of childhood favorites.

More Piggyback Songs - 195 more original songs.

Piggyback Songs for Infants and Toddlers - 160 original songs, for infants and toddlers.

Piggyback Songs in Praise of God - 185 original religious songs, sung to familiar tunes.

Piggyback Songs in Praise of Jesus - 240 more original religious songs.

Holiday Piggyback Songs - over 240 original holiday songs.

Animal Piggyback Songs - over 200 original songs about animals.

1•2•3 Art - over 200 open-ended art activities.

1•2•3 Games - 70 no-lose games to ages 2 to 8.

1•2•3 Colors - over 500 Color Day activities for young children.

1•2•3 Puppets - over 50 puppets to make for working with young children.

1•2•3 Murals - over 50 murals to make with children's open-ended art.

1•2•3 Books - over 20 beginning concept books to make for working with young children.

Teeny-Tiny Folktales - 15 folktales from around the world plus flannelboard patterns.

Short-Short Stories - 18 original stories plus seasonal activities.

Mini-Mini Musicals - 10 simple musicals, sung to familiar tunes.

Small World Celebrations - 16 holidays from around the world to celebrate with young children.

Special Day Celebrations - 55 mini celebrations for holidays and special events.

Yankee Doodle Birthday Celebrations - activity ideas for celebrating birthdays of 30 famous Americans.

"Cut & Tell" Scissor Stories for Fall - 8 original stories plus patterns.

"Cut & Tell" Scissor Stories for Winter - 8 original stories plus patterns.

"Cut & Tell" Scissor Stories for Spring - 8 original stories plus patterns.

Seasonal Fun - 50 two-sided reproducible parent flyers.

Theme-A-Saurus - the great big book of mini teaching themes.

Theme-A-Saurus II - the great big book of more mini teaching themes.

Alphabet and Number Rhymes - reproducible take-home books.

Color, Shape & Season Rhymes - reproducible take-home books.

Object Rhymes - reproducible take-home books about seasonal objects such as hearts, pumpkins and turkeys.

Animal Rhymes - reproducible pre-reading books using repetition and rhyme about animals.

Our World - more than 120 easy environmental activities.

"Mix & Match" Animal Patterns - multi-sized patterns for 58 different animals.

"Mix & Match" Everyday Patterns - multi-sized patterns for 58 different everyday objects.

"Mix & Match" Nature Patterns - multi-sized patterns for 58 different nature objects.

Available at school supply stores and parent/teacher stores or write for our *FREE* catalog.

Warren Publishing House, Inc. • P.O. Box 2250, Dept. B • Everett, WA 98203